Home is the natural habitat for human beings and has always been our primary school and church; it's where we learn to love learning and love God. Winfield Bevins has given families a valuable resource for forming the habits of the soul for every age, and forming those habits with our most primary relationships.

—Gloria Gaither
accomplished songwriter, author, and speaker

Living Room Liturgy draws deeply on Scripture and the riches of the church to help give us words for worship at home. I can't wait to use it on the sofa with my family!

—Beth Felker Jones
Professor of Theology
Wheaton College

I love this book of prayers for the home! I've valued using "A Liturgy for Times of Trouble" during the lockdown, and prayed "A Liturgy for Planting a Tree" with my son Isaac after moving a tree sapling to a new permanent home in our garden. This is a great resource, helping us to pray.

—Matthew Porter
Vicar of The Belfrey, York, UK
and author of *A-Z of Prayer*

The deep Christian traditions invite us to reimagine the home as a "little school of prayer." This liturgically accessible resource can guide households to once again insource discipleship between fathers and daughters, mothers and sons, and families of all shapes and sizes. I highly recommend Winfield's new book of liturgy for the home.

—A. J. Sherill
Pastor of Mars Hill Bible Church
and author of *Enneagram and Spiritual Formation*

This is absolutely brilliant. What a gift this book will be as churches continue to be dispersed into people's homes.

—Glenn Packium
Pastor of New Life Downtown
and author of *Blessed Broken Given*

For millennia the people of God have valued the home as a primary place of Christian discipleship. *Living Room Liturgy* recognizes this conviction and offers essential resources for cultivating the home as a place of prayer and praise. The book not only contains liturgical treasures presented in an accessible way, but it also holds great potential for revival through domestic means.

—Jonathan A. Powers
Assistant Professor of Worship
Asbury Theological Seminary

Winfield has mindfully curated this work to provide holy spaces from our homes, communities, and wherever we find ourselves. These rhythms echo from the best of our past and could gently and peacefully guide our spiritual future. Healthy spiritual practices eventually bring us to be the non-anxious presence the world continually needs.

—Fr. Chad E. Jarnagin
Author of *Learning to Be: Reconstructing Peace & Spiritual Health*

Living Room Liturgy is an incredibly helpful book of everyday liturgies that families and individuals can use for all liturgical seasons *and* seasons of life. It is a delight to find sets of liturgy and prayers that are straightforward and simple enough to understand for times when we may not have the words of a prayer to offer up ourselves. *Living Room Liturgy* challenges those who so long to be shaped by prayer and Scripture to take that first step because of its accessibility alone. Beautifully written, crafted, and theologically rich, Winfield's work douses us in daily Scripture and godly orientation so our souls can be steadied on the promises of Christ.

—Rachel Wilhelm
Author of *Songs of Lament*
and United States team leader for United Adoration

Winfield Bevins has written a book on liturgy that is truly a gift for people searching for consistent rhythms of prayer and families seeking to follow the way of Jesus. This book is particularly useful to transform ordinary moments at home into sacred encounters with the living God.

—Rusty Graves
Seacoast Church, Charleston, SC

I grew up in a home that gathered daily for "family altar." Our parents collected my brothers and me into our small parsonage living room to read Scripture and pray; sometimes we sang. Looking back, we now realize that those living room moments formed us deeply. *Living Room Liturgy* is a gift to a new wave of families seeking to fan the flame at the family altar.

—Constance M. Cherry
Professor of Worship and Pastoral Ministry at Indiana Wesleyan University
Pastor of Grant United Methodist Church

Liturgy, as "the work of the people," has often found itself within postmodernity in a similar position as the prodigal son. In *Living Room Liturgy*, Dr. Bevins reminds us of the familial origins of both the church's catechetical tradition and its pastoral vocation toward prayer and worship. This book not only allows liturgy to dust itself off and return to its proper place, the home, but also empowers those within the family dynamic to receive and embrace the long-lost experience of home worship.

—The Right Rev. Emilio Alvarez, PhD
Institute for Paleo-Orthodox Christian Studies

LIVING ROOM

LITURGY

Copyright 2020 by Winfield Bevins

All rights reserved. No part of this publication may be reproduced, stored in a retrieval system, or transmitted, in any form or by any means—electronic, mechanical, photocopying, recording, or otherwise—without prior written permission, except for brief quotations in critical reviews or articles.

Scripture quotations are taken from the Holy Bible, New International Version®, NIV® Copyright © 1973, 1978, 1984, 2011 by Biblica, Inc.™ Used by permission of Zondervan. All rights reserved worldwide. www.zondervan.com The "NIV" and "New International Version" are trademarks registered in the United States Patent and Trademark Office by Biblica, Inc.™ All rights reserved worldwide.

Printed in the United States of America

Cover and page design by Nick Perreault
Page layout by PerfecType, Nashville, Tennessee

Bevins, Winfield H.
   Living room liturgy : a book of worship for the home / Winfield Bevins. - Franklin, Tennessee : Seedbed Publishing, ©2020.
      pages ; cm.
         ISBN 9781628247978 (hardcover)
         ISBN 9781628248036 (Mobi)
         ISBN 9781628248272 (ePub)
         ISBN 9781628248289 (uPDF)
      1. Families--Prayers and devotions. 2. Liturgies.   I. Title.

BV255.B49 2020   249   2020948396

SEEDBED PUBLISHING
Franklin, Tennessee
seedbed.com

In loving memory
of my mother, Jane Craig Lewis
(1937–2020)

Contents

Introduction	xv

Part 1: For Daily Prayer — 3
A Liturgy for the Morning	5
A Liturgy for the Evening	7

Part 2: For Ordinary Life — 9
A Liturgy for a New Pet	11
A Liturgy for a Home Blessing	13
A Liturgy for a Family Blessing	15
A Liturgy for Loved Ones	17
A Liturgy for a Meal Blessing	19
A Liturgy for the Gift of Friendship	21
A Liturgy for a Small Group	23
A Liturgy for Reading the Scriptures	25
A Liturgy for a New Beginning	27
A Liturgy for the Beginning of a Journey	29
A Liturgy for Guidance and Direction	31
A Liturgy for the Good Earth	33
A Liturgy for Spiritual Renewal	35
A Liturgy for Rest	37
A Liturgy for Mission	39
A Liturgy for the Garden	41
A Liturgy for Peace in the World	43

Part 3: For Special Occasions — 45
A Liturgy for the Beginning of School	47
A Liturgy for a Birthday	49
A Liturgy for the Gift of a Child	51
A Liturgy for Adopting a Child	53
A Liturgy for a Wedding Anniversary	55
A Liturgy for Graduation	57
A Liturgy for Baptism	59
A Liturgy for Confirmation	61

CONTENTS

A Liturgy in Celebration of Diversity	63
A Liturgy for Planting a Tree	65
A Liturgy for a Love Feast	67

Part 4: For Difficult Seasons — 69

A Liturgy for Spiritual Warfare	71
A Liturgy for Overcoming Fear	73
A Liturgy for Things You Cannot Change	75
A Liturgy for Those Who Mourn	77
A Liturgy for the Elderly	79
A Liturgy for Lament	81
A Liturgy for Justice and Peace	83
A Liturgy for the Loss of Work	85
A Liturgy for the Depressed and Downcast	87
A Liturgy for the Poor and Neglected	89
A Liturgy for the Death of a Loved One	91
A Liturgy for Those with Addiction	93
A Liturgy for God's Healing	95
A Liturgy for Times of Trouble	97
A Liturgy for Times of Natural Disaster	99
A Liturgy for Social Conflict and Distress	101

Part 5: For Holy Days and Holidays — 103

A Liturgy for Advent	105
A Liturgy for Christmas	107
A Liturgy for Epiphany	109
A Liturgy for Lent	111
A Liturgy for Holy Week	113
A Liturgy for Easter	115
A Liturgy for Pentecost	117
A Liturgy for Thanksgiving	119
A Liturgy for New Year	121
A Liturgy for All Saints' Day	123
A Liturgy for St. Patrick's Day	125
A Liturgy for the Advent Wreath	127

CONTENTS

Part 6: Calls and Responses   131
The Beatitudes   133
A General Intercession   134
Affirming the Faith   136
For Thanksgiving   137
For God's Deliverance   138
For the Beginning of Lent   140
For Pentecost   143
A Franciscan Litany for Peace   144

Part 7: Table Blessings   145
Contemporary Blessings   147
Traditional Blessings   148

Part 8: Prayers of the Saints   149

Recommended Reading   157

Introduction

We are all familiar with the phrase, "Home is where the heart is." What if I told you that your home was more than just a mere house? Whether you realize it or not, your home is a domestic church. The English word "domestic" comes from the Latin *domesticus*, which refers to house, home, family, or household. The term "domestic" was used by the early church to describe the home as a "little church." The earliest Christians simply worshiped in ordinary people's homes. St. John Chrysostom (AD 349-407) once said, "Indeed, a house is a little church."[1] This reminds us that the home can be a place of Christian worship. Worship doesn't just happen within the four walls of a church building; it can also happen in our homes in the ordinary moments of everyday life.

This tradition did not end with the early church, but continued through the Reformation with Martin Luther and John Calvin, both of whom promoted family worship in the home and called upon parents to disciple their children. Later, Christians in England and America carried on the emphasis on family worship and discipleship. John Wesley wrote a *Collection of Prayers for Families*, which were to be used for morning and evening prayers throughout the week. The pastoral theologian Jonathan Edwards said that "Every Christian family ought to be as it were a little church."[2] Home can also be a place where worship and discipleship happens. This is a tradition that needs recovering.

Thinking about our homes as domestic churches is a radical paradigm shift for many of us in the West. However, many people are beginning to rediscover that worship is not just something we do on Sunday mornings, but can take place in the spaces that we live as well. Monsignor Renzo Bonetti stated: "The domestic church has its own liturgy that echoes and points to the universal church."[3] In other words, the rituals and practices of the home are liturgies that flow from the rituals and practices of the church. This means

---

1. St. John Chrysostom, Homily 20: On Ephesians 5:22-33, *St. John Chrysostom—On Marriage and Family Life* (Crestwood, NY: St. Vladimir's Seminary Press, 1991).
2. Jonathan Edwards, Sermons and Discourses, 1743-1758, eds. Wilson H. Kimnach and Harry S. Stout, vol. 25, *The Works of Jonathan Edwards* (New Haven; London: Yale University Press, 2006), 25:484.
3. Renzo Bonetti, *Signs of Love: Christian Liturgy in the Everyday Life of the Family* (Franklin, TN: Seedbed Publishing, 2012), 4.

that the home is also a place of Christian worship, learning, and discipleship. We bring the components of a worship service—which includes reading the Bible, praying, and singing—into our homes through liturgy.

Liturgy is a word that is often misunderstood. The English word "liturgy" comes from the Greek word *leitourgia,* which simply means "the work of the people." The origin of liturgy comes from the practice of worship in the early church, and the purpose is to unite the body of believers in the essential work of the people—the worship of the one true God. I use the term "liturgy" in the broadest sense to refer both to something we do together in corporate worship *and* to individual spiritual disciplines; practices that help root us daily in the worship of God.[4] There are a few reasons why I think liturgy can be helpful for the home.

Liturgy can help us slow down and celebrate the different seasons of life. What do I mean by this? The book of Ecclesiastes reminds us that, "There is a time for everything, and a season for every activity under the heavens" (Eccl. 3:1). From life to death, each season is unique and different and requires its own celebration, anticipation, mourning, reflection, and prayer. However, there are times when we simply don't have the words to express ourselves in prayer. When we don't know how to pray or when we need encouragement to pray during these moments, liturgy can help us. Liturgy can inspire and encourage us whenever we find ourselves at a loss for words or when our desire to pray is not there. Liturgy reminds us that life is rhythmic and that we need to honor God in all the seasons of life. Through liturgy we are able to acknowledge God's lordship in both the high and the low times of our lives.

Liturgy can also help us worship with others in a common way. "Common" doesn't mean something that is ordinary; rather, it means something that is shared in common with others. "Common" is also the root of the word "community" and refers to something we do or share together. By worshiping and praying in a common way through liturgy, we find that we are never really praying alone. Liturgy brings us together in worship by using common words and prayers that we speak together. Whether we are alone in a room or gathered with others in a small group, our prayers are united with believers both past and present. This is what theologian Scot McKnight describes in *Praying with the Church,* where he distinguishes between praying *in* the

---

4. See Winfield Bevins, *Ever Ancient, Ever New: The Allure of Liturgy for a New Generation* (Grand Rapids, MI: Zondervan, 2019).

INTRODUCTION

church and *with* the church. Liturgy gives us a common worship that unites us with those around us and with other believers around the world who are praying the same rhythm of prayers throughout the day.

Liturgy can also help us turn the ordinary places in our home into holy places. Today, the ordinary places that we inhabit most such as the family table, the living room, or even the car can become places of prayer and worship. Liturgy can help our homes become sacred places of hospitality and thanksgiving as we gather together to break bread, share stories, and give thanks. Something as ordinary as a bowl of soup or a grilled cheese sandwich can become a sacrament if it is made and received with love. How beautiful would it be if we offered up the ordinary times of the day and the spaces of our homes for the glory of God?

As you use these liturgies, I want to encourage you to set aside the ordinary places in your home for worship and prayer. Gather together in your kitchen, living room, or the backyard. Any place will do, as long as it is set apart for the Lord. These ordinary places can be transformed into holy places—or, as the Celtic Christians would call them, "thin places"—where we can meet with God. The regular moments of our days can become holy moments when consecrated to the Lord.

HOW TO USE THIS BOOK

Living Room Liturgy was written to help you worship in the everyday moments of life in your home. It contains liturgies and shorter prayers that can be used while enjoying a morning cup of coffee, at the dinner table, while you're spending time with your loved ones in your living room, or in the evenings at your children's bedsides before they fall asleep. This book is designed to be used in ordinary times throughout the day and for special occasions throughout the year. In putting this book together, I have carefully crafted each liturgy, selecting the scriptures, and I have written many of the prayers myself. However, some of the prayers have been drawn from several different sources, in particular, the *Book of Common Prayer*.[5] Some of them are very old, while others are new. It is important to say that these liturgies and

---

5. The *Book of Common Prayer* has been read by millions around the world and still influences Christians today; it is one of the most beautiful prayer books ever composed. A few years ago, I discovered the *Book of Common Prayer*, and a whole new world opened up to me. There are various versions, including the 1979, and the most recent 2019 version by the Anglican Church in North America.

INTRODUCTION

prayers do not belong to any one tradition, but they belong to all of us. I have written this book for Christians from various backgrounds who are looking for a way to bring liturgy into the home. I believe that we can all draw from the richness of the liturgical tradition of the church for today.

The book is divided into several sections that are easy to navigate. The first section is the daily prayer that contains liturgies that can be used for morning and evening prayer. The second section contains liturgies for ordinary life, such as blessing a home or a new beginning. The third section is for special occasions, from starting school to commemorating a wedding anniversary. The fourth section offers liturgies for difficult seasons of life ranging from the death of a loved one to a liturgy for healing. The fifth section offers liturgies that celebrate holy days and holidays throughout the Christian year, such as Christmas and Easter. The sixth section contains several calls and responses. The seventh section has a collection of table blessings that can be prayed around the family table. The final section contains a selection of prayers from various historic saints; these ancient prayers are timeless and will inspire you to emulate the faith of great saints who have gone before us.

Living Room Liturgy is a versatile book of worship that can be used by individuals, families, or small groups. In fact, I have personally used these liturgies and prayers in all three ways in various places in our home.

If you are using it by yourself, prayerfully read the liturgies alone. As you pray them, imagine joining your voice with other believers who are praying the same prayers.

When using these liturgies and prayers in a small group or as a family, select a person or persons to read the prayers and scriptures as the "Leader." Then, the sections that are labeled "People" can be read aloud by the rest of the group. Ideally, whether young or old, every member of the family can share in these prayers.

Each liturgy follows a similar pattern: opening, Scripture, prayer, reflection, the Lord's Prayer, and a closing. Finally, these are not official liturgies of the church, so feel free to make them personal. Use them at your own pace, add songs or additional scriptures, or pray additional prayers. This is, after all, *Living Room Liturgy*, so make it your own! May God bless you as you use these liturgies in your everyday life, especially in your home.

Winfield Bevins
Eastertide, 2020

LIVING ROOM

LITURGY

// Part 1
For Daily Prayer

A Liturgy for the Morning

OPENING

Leader: This is the day that the Lord has made.
People: **We will rejoice and be glad in it.**

SCRIPTURE

Read one of the following scriptures to prepare your heart for morning prayer.

- SUN I rejoiced with those who said to me, "Let us go to the house of the Lord." (Ps. 122:1)
- MON May these words of my mouth and this meditation of my heart be pleasing in your sight, Lord, my Rock and my Redeemer. (Ps. 19:14)
- TUE Send me your light and your faithful care, let them lead me; let them bring me to your holy mountain, to the place where you dwell. (Ps. 43:3)
- WED The Lord is in his holy temple; let all the earth be silent before him. (Hab. 2:20)
- THU "Yet a time is coming and has now come when the true worshipers will worship the Father in the Spirit and in truth, for they are the kind of worshipers the Father seeks." (John 4:23)
- FRI For this is what the high and exalted One says—he who lives forever, whose name is holy: "I live in a high and holy place, but also with the one who is contrite and lowly in spirit, to revive the spirit of the lowly and to revive the heart of the contrite." (Isa. 57:15)
- SAT Give praise to the Lord, proclaim his name; make known among the nations what he has done. (Ps. 105:1)

Leader: The Word of the Lord.
People: **Thanks be to God.**

PRAYER

Leader: The Lord be with you.
People: **And also with you.**
Leader: Let us pray.

Dear Lord, you have brought us in safety to this new day;
grant us courage and patience to do what we need to do today;
let our confidence not rest in our own understanding, but in your
    guiding hand;
let our desires not be for our own comfort,
but for the joy of your kingdom now and forever. Amen.

THE LORD'S PRAYER

Our Father, who art in heaven,
    hallowed be thy name.
    thy kingdom come,
    thy will be done
    on earth as it is in heaven.
Give us this day our daily bread.
And forgive us our trespasses,
    as we forgive those who trespass against us.
And lead us not into temptation,
    but deliver us from evil.
For thine is the kingdom,
    and the power,
    and the glory, forever. Amen.

PRAY FOR SPECIAL NEEDS

*Take some time to pray for the needs of your family, friends,
neighbors, local community, nation, and the world. Let
the Spirit lead you and guide you as you pray.*

CLOSING

Leader: Let us bless the Lord whose mercies are new every morning.
People: **Thanks be to God.**

A Liturgy for the Evening

OPENING ACCLAMATION

Leader: Our help is in the name of the Lord.
People: **The maker of heaven and earth.**

SCRIPTURE

Read one of the following scriptures to prepare your heart for evening prayer.

- SUN May my prayer be set before you like incense; may the lifting up of my hands be like the evening sacrifice. (Ps. 141:2)

- MON Grace and peace to you from God our Father and the Lord Jesus Christ. (Phil. 1:2)

- TUE Worship the LORD in the splendor of his holiness; tremble before him, all the earth. (Ps. 96:9)

- WED The day is yours, and yours also the night; you established the sun and moon. It was you who set all the boundaries of the earth; you made both summer and winter. (Ps. 74:16-17)

- THU I will praise the LORD, who counsels me; even at night my heart instructs me. I keep my eyes always on the LORD. With him at my right hand, I will not be shaken. (Ps. 16:7-8)

- FRI He who made the Pleiades and Orion, who turns midnight into dawn and darkens day into night, who calls for the waters of the sea and pours them out over the face of the land—the LORD is his name. (Amos 5:8)

- SAT If I say, "Surely the darkness will hide me and the light become night around me," even the darkness will not be dark to you; the night will shine like the day, for darkness is as light to you. (Ps. 139:11-12)

Leader: The Word of the Lord.
People: **Thanks be to God.**

PRAYER

Leader: The Lord be with you.
People: **And also with you.**
Leader: Let us pray.

Keep watch, dear Lord,
with those who work, or watch,
or weep this night,
and give your angels charge over those who sleep.
Tend the sick, Lord Christ;
give rest to the weary, bless the dying,
soothe the suffering, pity the afflicted, shield the joyous;
and all for your love's sake. Amen.

THE LORD'S PRAYER

Our Father, who art in heaven,
   hallowed be thy name.
   thy kingdom come,
   thy will be done
     on earth as it is in heaven.
Give us this day our daily bread.
And forgive us our trespasses,
   as we forgive those who trespass against us.
And lead us not into temptation,
   but deliver us from evil.
For thine is the kingdom,
   and the power,
   and the glory, forever. Amen.

PRAY FOR SPECIAL NEEDS

Take some time to pray for the needs of your family, friends, neighbors, local community, nation, and the world. Let the Spirit lead you and guide you as you pray.

CLOSING

Leader: Guide us waking, O Lord, and guard us sleeping.
People: **That awake we may watch with Christ, and asleep we may rest in peace.**

Part 2
For Ordinary Life

A Liturgy for a New Pet

OPENING

Leader: God made the animals according to their kinds.
People: And God saw that it was good.

SCRIPTURE

And God said, "Let the water teem with living creatures, and let birds fly above the earth across the vault of the sky." So God created the great creatures of the sea and every living thing with which the water teems and that moves about in it, according to their kinds, and every winged bird according to its kind. And God saw that it was good. God blessed them and said, "Be fruitful and increase in number and fill the water in the seas, and let the birds increase on the earth." And there was evening, and there was morning—the fifth day. And God said, "Let the land produce living creatures according to their kinds: the livestock, the creatures that move along the ground, and the wild animals, each according to its kind." And it was so. God made the wild animals according to their kinds, the livestock according to their kinds, and all the creatures that move along the ground according to their kinds. And God saw that it was good. (Gen. 1:20–25)

Leader: The Word of the Lord.
People: Thanks be to God.

PRAYER

Leader: The Lord be with you.
People: And also with you.
Leader: Let us pray.

Dear Lord, thank you for the blessing of our new pet, _____ (insert pet's name). We look forward to all of the memorable moments that are ahead. We recognize this new responsibility and we pray that we can tend to our new friend with great care. May he/she be kept in health and may our time together be filled with much companionship, joy, and love for many years to come. It's in your name we pray, amen.

REFLECTION

At this time, you may take a few minutes for a short reflection or personal prayer that goes along with the theme of the day.

THE LORD'S PRAYER

Our Father, who art in heaven,
  hallowed be thy name.
  thy kingdom come,
  thy will be done
  on earth as it is in heaven.
Give us this day our daily bread.
And forgive us our trespasses,
  as we forgive those who trespass against us.
And lead us not into temptation,
  but deliver us from evil.
For thine is the kingdom,
  and the power,
  and the glory, forever. Amen.

CLOSING

Leader: Let us bless the Lord for our new pet.
People: **Thanks be to God.**

A Liturgy for a Home Blessing

OPENING

Leader: Unless the Lord builds the house.
People: **Those who build it labor in vain.**

SCRIPTURE

"Why do you call me, 'Lord, Lord,' and do not do what I say? As for everyone who comes to me and hears my words and puts them into practice, I will show you what they are like. They are like a man building a house, who dug down deep and laid the foundation on rock. When a flood came, the torrent struck that house but could not shake it, because it was well built. But the one who hears my words and does not put them into practice is like a man who built a house on the ground without a foundation. The moment the torrent struck that house, it collapsed and its destruction was complete." (Luke 6:46–49)

Leader: The Word of the Lord.
People: **Thanks be to God.**

PRAYER

Leader: The Lord be with you.
People: **And also with you.**
Leader: Let us pray.

Heavenly Father, we pray that you would bless this house. Bless the feet that walk here, bless the hearts of those who lie down to sleep here. Would everyone who comes through the door of this home feel your love and your goodness. May this place be filled with joy, peace, and love, and may every need within this home be provided for. All this we ask through Jesus Christ our Lord, amen.

REFLECTION

At this time, you may take a few minutes for a short reflection or personal prayer that goes along with the theme of the day.

THE LORD'S PRAYER

Our Father, who art in heaven,
   hallowed be thy name.
   thy kingdom come,
   thy will be done
   on earth as it is in heaven.
Give us this day our daily bread.
And forgive us our trespasses,
   as we forgive those who trespass against us.
And lead us not into temptation,
   but deliver us from evil.
For thine is the kingdom,
   and the power,
   and the glory, forever. Amen.

CLOSING

Leader: Let us bless the Lord for this new house.
People: **Thanks be to God.**

A Liturgy for a Family Blessing

OPENING

Leader: Where two or three gather in your name.
People: There are you in the midst.

SCRIPTURE

But from everlasting to everlasting
   the Lord's love is with those who fear him,
   and his righteousness with their children's children—
with those who keep his covenant
   and remember to obey his precepts. (Ps. 103:17-18)

Leader: The Word of the Lord.
People: Thanks be to God.

PRAYER

Leader: The Lord be with you.
People: And also with you.
Leader: Let us pray.

Dear God, bless our home, we pray, that your love may rest upon us, and that your presence may dwell with us. May we all grow in grace and in the knowledge of you, our Lord and Savior. Teach us to love one another as you have commanded. Help us to bear one another's burdens in fulfillment of your law, O blessed Jesus, who with the Father and the Holy Spirit live and reign, one God, forever and ever. Amen.

REFLECTION

At this time, you may take a few minutes for a short reflection or personal prayer that goes along with the theme of the day.

THE LORD'S PRAYER

Our Father, who art in heaven,
   hallowed be thy name.

thy kingdom come,
thy will be done
on earth as it is in heaven.
Give us this day our daily bread.
And forgive us our trespasses,
    as we forgive those who trespass against us.
And lead us not into temptation,
    but deliver us from evil.
For thine is the kingdom,
    and the power,
    and the glory, forever. Amen.

CLOSING

Leader: Let us bless the Lord for our family.
People: **Thanks be to God.**

A Liturgy for Loved Ones

OPENING

Leader: I give thanks to my God always for you.
People: **Because of the grace of God.**

SCRIPTURE

Grace and peace to you from God our Father and the Lord Jesus Christ. I thank my God every time I remember you. In all my prayers for all of you, I always pray with joy because of your partnership in the gospel from the first day until now, being confident of this, that he who began a good work in you will carry it on to completion until the day of Christ Jesus. It is right for me to feel this way about all of you, since I have you in my heart and, whether I am in chains or defending and confirming the gospel, all of you share in God's grace with me. (Phil. 1:2-7)

Leader: The Word of the Lord.
People: **Thanks be to God.**

PRAYER

Leader: The Lord be with you.
People: **And also with you.**
Leader: Let us pray.

O loving Father, we commend to your gracious keeping all who are near and dear to us. Have mercy upon any who are sick, and comfort those who are in pain, anxiety, or sorrow. Awaken all who are careless about eternal things. Bless those who are young and in health, that they may give the days of their strength to you. Comfort the aged and infirm, that your peace may rest upon them. Hallow the ties of kindred, that we may help and not hinder one another in all the good works that you have prepared for us to walk in, through Jesus Christ our Lord. Amen.

REFLECTION

At this time, you may take a few minutes for a short reflection or personal prayer that goes along with the theme of the day.

THE LORD'S PRAYER

Our Father, who art in heaven,
    hallowed be thy name.
    thy kingdom come,
    thy will be done
    on earth as it is in heaven.
Give us this day our daily bread.
And forgive us our trespasses,
    as we forgive those who trespass against us.
And lead us not into temptation,
    but deliver us from evil.
For thine is the kingdom,
    and the power,
    and the glory, forever. Amen.

CLOSING

Leader: Let us bless the Lord for all those we love.
People: **Thanks be to God.**

A Liturgy for a Meal Blessing

OPENING

Leader: Jesus took bread, gave thanks, broke it.
People: **Then their eyes were opened and they recognized him.**

SCRIPTURE

As they approached the village to which they were going, Jesus continued on as if he were going farther. But they urged him strongly, "Stay with us, for it is nearly evening; the day is almost over." So he went in to stay with them. When he was at the table with them, he took bread, gave thanks, broke it and began to give it to them. Then their eyes were opened and they recognized him, and he disappeared from their sight. They asked each other, "Were not our hearts burning within us while he talked with us on the road and opened the Scriptures to us?" (Luke 24:28–32)

Leader: The Word of the Lord.
People: **Thanks be to God.**

PRAYER

Leader: The Lord be with you.
People: **And also with you.**
Leader: Let us pray.

Dear Lord Jesus, the Gospels remind us that you shared a meal to minister to people and to teach others important lessons about the kingdom of God. Come now, Lord, be our guest at our dinner table and be known to us in the breaking of bread. We thank you for providing us with a roof over our heads, for the good food before us, for those who prepared it, and for friends and family with whom to share it. We pray that you bless, O Lord, this food to our use and us to thy service, and keep us ever mindful of the needs of others. In Jesus' name, amen.

REFLECTION

At this time, you may take a few minutes for a short reflection or personal prayer that goes along with the theme of the day.

THE LORD'S PRAYER

Our Father, who art in heaven,
   hallowed be thy name.
   thy kingdom come,
   thy will be done
   on earth as it is in heaven.
Give us this day our daily bread.
And forgive us our trespasses,
   as we forgive those who trespass against us.
And lead us not into temptation,
   but deliver us from evil.
For thine is the kingdom,
   and the power,
   and the glory, forever. Amen.

CLOSING

Leader: Let us bless the Lord for the food before us.
People: **Thanks be to God.**

A Liturgy for the Gift of Friendship

OPENING

Leader: Two are better than one.
People: **If either of them falls down, one can help the other up.**

SCRIPTURE

Therefore, as God's chosen people, holy and dearly loved, clothe yourselves with compassion, kindness, humility, gentleness and patience. Bear with each other and forgive one another if any of you has a grievance against someone. Forgive as the Lord forgave you. And over all these virtues put on love, which binds them all together in perfect unity. (Col. 3:12–14)

Leader: The Word of the Lord.
People: **Thanks be to God.**

PRAYER

Leader: The Lord be with you.
People: **And also with you.**
Leader: Let us pray.

O God, you have blessed us with the gift of friendship. We thank you for such a blessing; for friends who love us, who share our joys and our sorrows, who laugh with us in celebration, who bear our pain, who need us as we need them, who weep as we weep, who hold us when words fail, and who give us the freedom to be ourselves. Bless our friends with health, wholeness, life, and love. Amen.

REFLECTION

At this time, you may take a few minutes for a short reflection or personal prayer that goes along with the theme of the day.

THE LORD'S PRAYER

Our Father, who art in heaven,
    hallowed be thy name.
    thy kingdom come,
    thy will be done
    on earth as it is in heaven.
Give us this day our daily bread.
And forgive us our trespasses,
    as we forgive those who trespass against us.
And lead us not into temptation,
    but deliver us from evil.
For thine is the kingdom,
    and the power,
    and the glory, forever. Amen.

CLOSING

Leader: Let us bless the Lord for the gift of friendship.
People: **Thanks be to God.**

A Liturgy for a Small Group

OPENING

Leader: Where two or three are gathered.
People: I am in their midst.

SCRIPTURE

Let us hold unswervingly to the hope we profess, for he who promised is faithful. And let us consider how we may spur one another on toward love and good deeds, not giving up meeting together, as some are in the habit of doing, but encouraging one another—and all the more as you see the Day approaching. (Heb. 10:23-25)

Leader: The Word of the Lord.
People: Thanks be to God.

PRAYER

Leader: The Lord be with you.
People: And also with you.
Leader: Let us pray.

Dear Lord, you have created us for fellowship and community. The earliest Christians devoted themselves to the apostles' teaching and to fellowship, to the breaking of bread and to prayer, and they broke bread in their homes and ate together with glad and sincere hearts. We thank you for the gift of fellowship, and may we who gather together in this small group follow in their example and gather with other Christians for mutual prayer, support, and encouragement. Unite us together in the bonds of fellowship and use our small group as a means of grace that we may draw closer to you. Amen.

REFLECTION

At this time, you may take a few minutes for a short reflection or personal prayer that goes along with the theme of the day.

THE LORD'S PRAYER

Our Father, who art in heaven,
   hallowed be thy name.
   thy kingdom come,
   thy will be done
   on earth as it is in heaven.
Give us this day our daily bread.
And forgive us our trespasses,
   as we forgive those who trespass against us.
And lead us not into temptation,
   but deliver us from evil.
For thine is the kingdom,
   and the power,
   and the glory, forever. Amen.

CLOSING

Leader: Let us bless the Lord for the gift of our small group.
People: **Thanks be to God.**

A Liturgy for Reading the Scriptures

OPENING

Leader: For the Word of God is alive and active.
People: **Sharper than any two-edged sword.**

SCRIPTURE

But as for you, continue in what you have learned and have become convinced of, because you know those from whom you learned it, and how from infancy you have known the Holy Scriptures, which are able to make you wise for salvation through faith in Christ Jesus. All Scripture is God-breathed and is useful for teaching, rebuking, correcting and training in righteousness, so that the servant of God may be thoroughly equipped for every good work. (2 Tim. 3:14–17)

Leader: The Word of the Lord.
People: **Thanks be to God.**

PRAYER

Leader: The Lord be with you.
People: **And also with you.**
Leader: Let us pray.

Blessed Lord, who caused all Holy Scriptures to be written for our learning: Grant us so to hear them, read, mark, learn, and inwardly digest them, that by patience and the comfort of your Holy Word we may embrace and ever hold fast the blessed hope of everlasting life, which you have given us in our Savior Jesus Christ, who lives and reigns with you and the Holy Spirit, one God, forever and ever. Amen.

REFLECTION

At this time, you may take a few minutes for a short reflection or personal prayer that goes along with the theme of the day.

THE LORD'S PRAYER

Our Father, who art in heaven,
   hallowed be thy name.
   thy kingdom come,
   thy will be done
   on earth as it is in heaven.
Give us this day our daily bread.
And forgive us our trespasses,
   as we forgive those who trespass against us.
And lead us not into temptation,
   but deliver us from evil.
For thine is the kingdom,
   and the power,
   and the glory, forever. Amen.

CLOSING

Leader: Let us bless the Lord for the Word of God.
People: **Thanks be to God.**

A Liturgy for a New Beginning

OPENING

Leader: The old is gone.
People: **The new has come.**

SCRIPTURE

"Forget the former things;
  do not dwell on the past.
See, I am doing a new thing!
  Now it springs up; do you not perceive it?
I am making a way in the wilderness
  and streams in the wasteland." (Isa. 43:18-19)

Leader: The Word of the Lord.
People: **Thanks be to God.**

PRAYER

Leader: The Lord be with you.
People: **And also with you.**
Leader: Let us pray.

Dear Lord, you are the God of new beginnings and your Word tells us that you make all things new. Today, we ask that you would make us a new creation and that you would bless us with a new beginning. Help us to let go of the past and give us a fresh start and a new beginning today. As spring brings new life to the earth, so I pray that you would do a new thing in our life. We commit our lives, our love, and all that we have into your hands of love. Amen.

REFLECTION

At this time, you may take a few minutes for a short reflection or personal prayer that goes along with the theme of the day.

THE LORD'S PRAYER

Our Father, who art in heaven,
   hallowed be thy name.
   thy kingdom come,
   thy will be done
   on earth as it is in heaven.
Give us this day our daily bread.
And forgive us our trespasses,
   as we forgive those who trespass against us.
And lead us not into temptation,
   but deliver us from evil.
For thine is the kingdom,
   and the power,
   and the glory, forever. Amen.

CLOSING

Leader: Let us bless the Lord for new beginnings.
People: **Thanks be to God.**

A Liturgy for the Beginning of a Journey

OPENING

Leader: You will be blessed when you come in.
People: **And blessed when you go out.**

SCRIPTURE

I lift up my eyes to the mountains—
  where does my help come from?
My help comes from the Lord,
  the Maker of heaven and earth.

He will not let your foot slip—
  he who watches over you will not slumber;
indeed, he who watches over Israel
  will neither slumber nor sleep.

The Lord watches over you—
  the Lord is your shade at your right hand;
the sun will not harm you by day,
  nor the moon by night.

The Lord will keep you from all harm—
  he will watch over your life;
the Lord will watch over your coming and going
  both now and forevermore. (Ps. 121:1–8)

Leader: The Word of the Lord.
People: **Thanks be to God.**

PRAYER

Leader: The Lord be with you.
People: **And also with you.**
Leader: Let us pray.

O God, you have called us to live in this world as a pilgrim people, daily walking the journey of faith. Today, we begin a new journey. Our heavenly Father, whose glory fills the whole creation, and whose presence we find wherever we go, preserve us as we travel; surround us with your loving care; protect us from every danger; and bring us in safety to our journey's end, through Jesus Christ our Lord. Amen.

REFLECTION

At this time, you may take a few minutes for a short reflection or personal prayer that goes along with the theme of the day.

THE LORD'S PRAYER

Our Father, who art in heaven,
   hallowed be thy name.
   thy kingdom come,
   thy will be done
   on earth as it is in heaven.
Give us this day our daily bread.
And forgive us our trespasses,
   as we forgive those who trespass against us.
And lead us not into temptation,
   but deliver us from evil.
For thine is the kingdom,
   and the power,
   and the glory, forever. Amen.

CLOSING

Leader: Let us bless the Lord for the journey of faith.
People: **Thanks be to God.**

A Liturgy for Guidance and Direction

OPENING

Leader: Thy Word is a lamp unto my feet.
People: **And light unto my path.**

SCRIPTURE

The Lord is my shepherd, I lack nothing.
   He makes me lie down in green pastures,
he leads me beside quiet waters,
   he refreshes my soul.
He guides me along the right paths
   for his name's sake.
Even though I walk
   through the darkest valley,
I will fear no evil,
   for you are with me;
your rod and your staff,
   they comfort me.

You prepare a table before me
   in the presence of my enemies.
You anoint my head with oil;
   my cup overflows.
Surely your goodness and love will follow me
   all the days of my life,
and I will dwell in the house of the Lord
   forever. (Ps. 23)

Leader: The Word of the Lord.
People: **Thanks be to God.**

PRAYER

Leader: The Lord be with you.
People: **And also with you.**
Leader: Let us pray.

Heavenly Father, in you we live and move and have our being. When the way is dark and we cannot see the road ahead, we humbly pray you guide and govern us by your Holy Spirit, that in all the cares and occupations of our life we may not forget you, but may remember that we are ever walking in your sight; through Jesus Christ our Lord. Amen.

REFLECTION

At this time, you may take a few minutes for a short reflection or personal prayer that goes along with the theme of the day.

THE LORD'S PRAYER

Our Father, who art in heaven,
   hallowed be thy name.
   thy kingdom come,
   thy will be done
   on earth as it is in heaven.
Give us this day our daily bread.
And forgive us our trespasses,
   as we forgive those who trespass against us.
And lead us not into temptation,
   but deliver us from evil.
For thine is the kingdom,
   and the power,
   and the glory, forever. Amen.

CLOSING

Leader: Let us bless the Lord who guides our paths.
People: **Thanks be to God.**

A Liturgy for the Good Earth

OPENING

Leader: The earth is the Lord's for he made it.
People: **O Come, let us adore him.**

SCRIPTURE

The heavens declare the glory of God;
    the skies proclaim the work of his hands.
Day after day they pour forth speech;
    night after night they reveal knowledge.
They have no speech, they use no words;
    no sound is heard from them.
Yet their voice goes out into all the earth,
    their words to the ends of the world.
In the heavens God has pitched a tent for the sun.
It is like a bridegroom coming out of his chamber,
    like a champion rejoicing to run his course.
It rises at one end of the heavens
    and makes its circuit to the other;
    nothing is deprived of its warmth. (Ps. 19:1–6)

Leader: The Word of the Lord.
People: **Thanks be to God.**

PRAYER

Leader: The Lord be with you.
People: **And also with you.**
Leader: Let us pray.

O heavenly Father, who has filled the world with beauty, open our eyes to behold your gracious hand in all your works that, rejoicing in your whole creation, we may learn to serve you with gladness for the sake of him through whom all things were made, your Son Jesus Christ our Lord. We thank you for making the earth fruitful so that it might produce what is needed for life. Bless those who work in the fields, give us seasonable weather, and grant that we may all share the fruits of the earth, rejoicing in your goodness through Jesus Christ our Lord. Amen.

REFLECTION

At this time, you may take a few minutes for a short reflection or personal prayer that goes along with the theme of the day.

THE LORD'S PRAYER

Our Father, who art in heaven,
   hallowed be thy name.
   thy kingdom come,
   thy will be done
   on earth as it is in heaven.
Give us this day our daily bread.
And forgive us our trespasses,
   as we forgive those who trespass against us.
And lead us not into temptation,
   but deliver us from evil.
For thine is the kingdom,
   and the power,
   and the glory, forever. Amen.

CLOSING

Leader: Let us bless the Lord for the good earth.
People: **Thanks be to God.**

A Liturgy for Spiritual Renewal

OPENING

Leader: O Lord, our hearts are restless.
People: Until they find their rest in you.

SCRIPTURE

Create in me a pure heart, O God,
   and renew a steadfast spirit within me.
Do not cast me from your presence
   or take your Holy Spirit from me.
Restore to me the joy of your salvation
   and grant me a willing spirit, to sustain me. (Ps. 51:10–12)

Leader: The Word of the Lord.
People: Thanks be to God.

PRAYER

Leader: The Lord be with you.
People: And also with you.
Leader: Let us pray.

Almighty and eternal God, so draw our hearts to you, so guide our minds, so fill our imaginations, so control our wills, that we may be wholly yours, utterly dedicated unto you; and then use us, we pray, as you will, and always to your glory and the welfare of your people, through our Lord and Savior Jesus Christ. Amen.

REFLECTION

At this time, you may take a few minutes for a short reflection or personal prayer that goes along with the theme of the day.

THE LORD'S PRAYER

Our Father, who art in heaven,
   hallowed be thy name.

   thy kingdom come,
   thy will be done
   on earth as it is in heaven.
Give us this day our daily bread.
And forgive us our trespasses,
   as we forgive those who trespass against us.
And lead us not into temptation,
   but deliver us from evil.
For thine is the kingdom,
   and the power,
   and the glory, forever. Amen.

CLOSING

Leader: Let us bless the Lord for renewing our hearts.
People: **Thanks be to God.**

A Liturgy for Rest

OPENING

Leader: Come to me, all you who are weary and burdened.
People: **I will give you rest.**

SCRIPTURE

"Come to me, all you who are weary and burdened, and I will give you rest. Take my yoke upon you and learn from me, for I am gentle and humble in heart, and you will find rest for your souls. For my yoke is easy and my burden is light." (Matt. 11:28–30)

Leader: The Word of the Lord.
People: **Thanks be to God.**

PRAYER

Leader: The Lord be with you.
People: **And also with you.**
Leader: Let us pray.

Almighty God, you invite us to come to you in order that we may find rest for our weary souls. In the course of this busy life, give us times of refreshment and peace, and grant that we may so use our leisure to rebuild our bodies and renew our minds, that our spirits may be opened to the goodness of your creation, through Jesus Christ our Lord. Amen.

REFLECTION

At this time, you may take a few minutes for a short reflection or personal prayer that goes along with the theme of the day.

THE LORD'S PRAYER

Our Father, who art in heaven,
   hallowed be thy name.
   thy kingdom come,
   thy will be done

on earth as it is in heaven.
Give us this day our daily bread.
And forgive us our trespasses,
    as we forgive those who trespass against us.
And lead us not into temptation,
    but deliver us from evil.
For thine is the kingdom,
    and the power,
    and the glory, forever. Amen.

CLOSING

Leader: Let us bless the Lord who gives us rest.
People: **Thanks be to God.**

A Liturgy for Mission

OPENING

Leader: Peace be with you.
People: **As the Father sent me, so I send you.**

SCRIPTURE

Then Jesus came to them and said, "All authority in heaven and on earth has been given to me. Therefore go and make disciples of all nations, baptizing them in the name of the Father and of the Son and of the Holy Spirit, and teaching them to obey everything I have commanded you. And surely I am with you always, to the very end of the age." (Matt. 28:18–20)

Leader: The Word of the Lord.
People: **Thanks be to God.**

PRAYER

Leader: The Lord be with you.
People: **And also with you.**
Leader: Let us pray.

Almighty God our Savior, you desire that none should perish, and you have taught us through your Son that there is great joy in heaven over every sinner who repents. Grant that our hearts may ache for a lost and broken world. May your Holy Spirit work through our words, deeds, and prayers, that the lost may be found and the dead made alive, and that all your redeemed may rejoice around your throne; through Jesus Christ our Lord. Amen.

REFLECTION

At this time, you may take a few minutes for a short reflection or personal prayer that goes along with the theme of the day.

THE LORD'S PRAYER

Our Father, who art in heaven,
   hallowed be thy name.
   thy kingdom come,
   thy will be done
   on earth as it is in heaven.
Give us this day our daily bread.
And forgive us our trespasses,
   as we forgive those who trespass against us.
And lead us not into temptation,
   but deliver us from evil.
For thine is the kingdom,
   and the power,
   and the glory, forever. Amen.

CLOSING

Leader: Let us go in mission and share the good news of Jesus Christ!
People: Thanks be to God.

A Liturgy for the Garden

OPENING

Leader: So neither he who plants nor he who waters is anything,
People: **But only God who gives the growth.**

SCRIPTURE

He also said, "This is what the kingdom of God is like. A man scatters seed on the ground. Night and day, whether he sleeps or gets up, the seed sprouts and grows, though he does not know how. All by itself the soil produces grain—first the stalk, then the head, then the full kernel in the head. As soon as the grain is ripe, he puts the sickle to it, because the harvest has come."

Again he said, "What shall we say the kingdom of God is like, or what parable shall we use to describe it? It is like a mustard seed, which is the smallest of all seeds on earth. Yet when planted, it grows and becomes the largest of all garden plants, with such big branches that the birds can perch in its shade." (Mark 4:26–32)

Leader: The Word of the Lord.
People: **Thanks be to God.**

PRAYER

Leader: The Lord be with you.
People: **And also with you.**
Leader: Let us pray.

Most gracious God of creation, you made the earth a garden where we could walk and talk with you among the plants and animals. Lord, bless our garden, may it be a place of peace by day and by night, throughout each season of life. Meet us, we pray, in this garden. May it be a place of nourishment, refreshment, fellowship, and prayer. May you also make our lives a spiritual garden, that we may bear fruit for you. Give us grace to abide in Jesus Christ, the True Vine. Amen.

REFLECTION

At this time, you may take a few minutes for a short reflection or personal prayer that goes along with the theme of the day.

THE LORD'S PRAYER

Our Father, who art in heaven,
   hallowed be thy name.
   thy kingdom come,
   thy will be done
   on earth as it is in heaven.
Give us this day our daily bread.
And forgive us our trespasses,
   as we forgive those who trespass against us.
And lead us not into temptation,
   but deliver us from evil.
For thine is the kingdom,
   and the power,
   and the glory, forever. Amen.

CLOSING

Leader: Let us bless the Lord for giving us this garden.
People: **Thanks be to God.**

A Liturgy for Peace in the World

OPENING

Leader: I pray also for those who will believe in me
People: **That all of them may be one.**

SCRIPTURE

How good and pleasant it is
    when God's people live together in unity!

It is like precious oil poured on the head,
    running down on the beard,
running down on Aaron's beard,
    down on the collar of his robe.
It is as if the dew of Hermon
    were falling on Mount Zion.
For there the Lord bestows his blessing,
    even life forevermore. (Ps. 133:1–3)

Leader: The Word of the Lord.
People: **Thanks be to God.**

PRAYER

Leader: The Lord be with you.
People: **And also with you.**
Leader: Let us pray.

Eternal God, in whose perfect kingdom no sword is drawn but the sword of righteousness, no strength known but the strength of love: So mightily spread abroad your Spirit, that all peoples may be gathered under the banner of the Prince of Peace, to whom be dominion and glory, now and forever. Kindle, we pray, in the hearts of all people the true love of peace, and guide with your pure and peaceable wisdom those who take counsel for the nations of the earth, that in tranquility your kingdom may go forward, till the earth is filled with the knowledge of your love, through Jesus Christ our Lord. Amen.

REFLECTION

At this time, you may take a few minutes for a short reflection or personal prayer that goes along with the theme of the day.

THE LORD'S PRAYER

Our Father, who art in heaven,
    hallowed be thy name.
    thy kingdom come,
    thy will be done
    on earth as it is in heaven.
Give us this day our daily bread.
And forgive us our trespasses,
    as we forgive those who trespass against us.
And lead us not into temptation,
    but deliver us from evil.
For thine is the kingdom,
    and the power,
    and the glory, forever. Amen.

CLOSING

Leader: Let us bless the Lord for the gift of unity.
People: **Thanks be to God.**

Part 3
For Special Occasions

A Liturgy for the Beginning of School

OPENING

Leader: This is the day that the Lord has made.
People: **We will rejoice and be glad in it.**

SCRIPTURE

My son, If you accept my words
   and store up my commands within you,
turning your ear to wisdom
   and applying your heart to understanding—
indeed, if you call out for insight
   and cry aloud for understanding,
and if you look for it as for silver
   and search for it as for hidden treasure,
then you will understand the fear of the Lord
   and find the knowledge of God.
For the Lord gives wisdom;
   from his mouth come knowledge and understanding.
He holds success in store for the upright,
   he is a shield to those whose walk is blameless,
for he guards the course of the just
   and protects the way of his faithful ones. (Prov. 2:1–8)

Leader: The Word of the Lord.
People: **Thanks be to God.**

PRAYER

Leader: The Lord be with you.
People: **And also with you.**
Leader: Let us pray.

Our Father in heaven, would you be with our children today as they learn? We ask that you extend your sovereign hand of love, guidance, and protection to our children wherever they may go today and whatever the task before them may be. Grant them courage and wisdom when it is needed. May they learn and grow to fulfill the purposes that you have planned for them. Dear Lord, bless our children today and help them do their best. Teach them to be good stewards of all you have given them. Show them how to develop their talents, to find the path you have set before them, and to be courageous and adventurous to try new things and learn new skills. Show them the importance of learning, remembering that you are always with them, leading them as they acknowledge you daily. Amen.

REFLECTION

At this time, you may take a few minutes for a short reflection or personal prayer that goes along with the theme of the day.

THE LORD'S PRAYER

Our Father, who art in heaven,
   hallowed be thy name.
   thy kingdom come,
   thy will be done
   on earth as it is in heaven.
Give us this day our daily bread.
And forgive us our trespasses,
   as we forgive those who trespass against us.
And lead us not into temptation,
   but deliver us from evil.
For thine is the kingdom,
   and the power,
   and the glory, forever. Amen.

CLOSING

Leader: Let us bless the Lord.
People: Thanks be to God.

A Liturgy for a Birthday

OPENING

Leader: The Lord bless you and keep you.
People: **The Lord make his face shine upon you.**

SCRIPTURE

"For I know the plans I have for you," declares the Lord, "plans to prosper you and not to harm you, plans to give you hope and a future. Then you will call on me and come and pray to me, and I will listen to you. You will seek me and find me when you seek me with all your heart." (Jer. 29:11-13)

Leader: The Word of the Lord.
People: **Thanks be to God.**

PRAYER

Leader: The Lord be with you.
People: **And also with you.**
Leader: Let us pray.

Dear Lord, we thank you for _____ (insert name) and we celebrate the gift of his/her life today. As he/she begins another year, we ask that you would continue to guide him/her in your Word and help him/her trust in your goodness and grace. Bless him/her with every blessing. In Jesus' name we pray, amen.

REFLECTION

At this time, you may take a few minutes for a short reflection or personal prayer that goes along with the theme of the day.

THE LORD'S PRAYER

Our Father, who art in heaven,
   hallowed be thy name.
   thy kingdom come,

thy will be done
   on earth as it is in heaven.
Give us this day our daily bread.
And forgive us our trespasses,
   as we forgive those who trespass against us.
And lead us not into temptation,
   but deliver us from evil.
For thine is the kingdom,
   and the power,
   and the glory, forever. Amen.

CLOSING

Leader: Let us bless the Lord for the birth of _____ (insert name).
People: **Thanks be to God.**

Liturgy for the Gift of a Child

OPENING

Leader: Let the children come to me.
People: For such is the kingdom of God.

SCRIPTURE

"Can a mother forget the baby at her breast and have no compassion on the child she has borne? Though she may forget, I will not forget you! See, I have engraved you on the palms of my hands; your walls are ever before me." (Isa. 49:15–16)

Leader: The Word of the Lord.
People: Thanks be to God.

PRAYER

Leader: The Lord be with you.
People: And also with you.
Leader: Let us pray.

Heavenly Father, you sent your own Son into this world. We thank you for the life of this child, entrusted to our care. Help us to remember that we are all your children, and so to love and nurture him/her, that he/she may attain to that full stature intended for him/her in your eternal kingdom, for the sake of your dear Son, Jesus Christ our Lord. Amen.

or

God our Father, you see your children growing up in an unsteady and confusing world. Show them that your ways give more life than the ways of the world, and that following you is better than chasing after selfish goals. Help them to take failure, not as a measure of their worth, but as a chance for a new start. Give them strength to hold their faith in you, and to keep alive their joy in your creation, through Jesus Christ our Lord. Amen.

REFLECTION

At this time, you may take a few minutes for a short reflection or personal prayer that goes along with the theme of the day.

THE LORD'S PRAYER

Our Father, who art in heaven,
   hallowed be thy name.
   thy kingdom come,
   thy will be done
   on earth as it is in heaven.
Give us this day our daily bread.
And forgive us our trespasses,
   as we forgive those who trespass against us.
And lead us not into temptation,
   but deliver us from evil.
For thine is the kingdom,
   and the power,
   and the glory, forever. Amen.

DISMISSAL

Leader: Let us bless the Lord for our children.
People: **Thanks be to God.**

A Liturgy for Adopting a Child

OPENING

Leader: God is a father to the fatherless.
People: **God sets the lonely in families.**

SCRIPTURE

Praise be to the God and Father of our Lord Jesus Christ, who has blessed us in the heavenly realms with every spiritual blessing in Christ. For he chose us in him before the creation of the world to be holy and blameless in his sight. In love he predestined us for adoption to sonship through Jesus Christ, in accordance with his pleasure and will—to the praise of his glorious grace, which he has freely given us in the One he loves. In him we have redemption through his blood, the forgiveness of sins, in accordance with the riches of God's grace that he lavished on us. With all wisdom and understanding, he made known to us the mystery of his will according to his good pleasure, which he purposed in Christ, to be put into effect when the times reach their fulfillment—to bring unity to all things in heaven and on earth under Christ. (Eph. 1:3-10)

Leader: The Word of the Lord.
People: **Thanks be to God.**

PRAYER

Leader: The Lord be with you.
People: **And also with you.**
Leader: Let us pray.

Our heavenly Father, you have given us the Spirit of adoption, that we who were strangers might become members of the household of God. The adoption of a child is a joyous and solemn occasion in the life of a family, and an occasion for rejoicing in the church. It has pleased you, almighty God, our heavenly Father, to bless us with the gift of _____ (insert name). God, you have taught us through your blessed Son that whoever receives a little child in the name of Christ receives Christ himself. We give thanks for the blessing you have bestowed upon us in giving us this child. Confirm and give us calm strength and patient wisdom as we seek to bring this child to love all that is true and noble, just and pure, lovable and gracious, excellent and admirable, following the example of our Lord and Savior Jesus Christ. Amen.

REFLECTION

At this time, you may take a few minutes for a short reflection or personal prayer that goes along with the theme of the day.

THE LORD'S PRAYER

Our Father, who art in heaven,
   hallowed be thy name.
   thy kingdom come,
   thy will be done
   on earth as it is in heaven.
Give us this day our daily bread.
And forgive us our trespasses,
   as we forgive those who trespass against us.
And lead us not into temptation,
   but deliver us from evil.
For thine is the kingdom,
   and the power,
   and the glory, forever. Amen.

CLOSING

Leader: Let us bless the Lord for the gift of this child.
People: **Thanks be to God.**

A Liturgy for a Wedding Anniversary

OPENING

Leader: A man shall leave his father and mother and be joined to his wife.

People: **The two shall become one flesh.**

SCRIPTURE

Love is patient, love is kind. It does not envy, it does not boast, it is not proud. It does not dishonor others, it is not self-seeking, it is not easily angered, it keeps no record of wrongs. Love does not delight in evil but rejoices with the truth. It always protects, always trusts, always hopes, always perseveres. (1 Cor. 13:4-7)

Leader: The Word of the Lord.
People: **Thanks be to God.**

PRAYER

Leader: The Lord be with you.
People: **And also with you.**
Leader: Let us pray.

Lord, we thank you for all of the years that we have had together. Today, as we celebrate our anniversary, we ask that you will continue to bless us in the years ahead. Let our life together be one of love and forgiveness and may it be a help to other couples as they start on their own journeys into married life. Lord, we pray that you will honor our commitment to each other and to you by granting us many more years of happiness. Amen.

REFLECTION

At this time, you may take a few minutes for a short reflection or personal prayer that goes along with the theme of the day.

THE LORD'S PRAYER

Our Father, who art in heaven,
    hallowed be thy name.
    thy kingdom come,
    thy will be done
    on earth as it is in heaven.
Give us this day our daily bread.
And forgive us our trespasses,
    as we forgive those who trespass against us.
And lead us not into temptation,
    but deliver us from evil.
For thine is the kingdom,
    and the power,
    and the glory, forever. Amen.

CLOSING

Leader: Let us bless the Lord for our marriage vows.
People: **Thanks be to God.**

A Liturgy for Graduation

OPENING

Leader: This is the day that the Lord has made.
People: **We will rejoice and be glad in it.**

SCRIPTURE

So then, just as you received Christ Jesus as Lord, continue to live in him, rooted and built up in him, strengthened in the faith as you were taught, and overflowing with thankfulness. (Col. 2:6-7)

Leader: The Word of the Lord.
People: **Thanks be to God.**

PRAYER

Leader: The Lord be with you.
People: **And also with you.**
Leader: Let us pray.

Almighty God, today we celebrate the accomplishments of our graduate, _____ (insert name). He/she has worked very diligently, and we thank you for your provision, wisdom, and guidance for him/her along the way. May he/she continue to walk in your will in the days ahead. Please bless his/her life with faith, hope, and love, and please help him/her to use his/her gifts wisely, all for your glory, through Jesus Christ our Lord. Amen.

REFLECTION

At this time, you may take a few minutes for a short reflection or personal prayer that goes along with the theme of the day.

THE LORD'S PRAYER

Our Father, who art in heaven,
   hallowed be thy name.
   thy kingdom come,

thy will be done
   on earth as it is in heaven.
Give us this day our daily bread.
And forgive us our trespasses,
   as we forgive those who trespass against us.
And lead us not into temptation,
   but deliver us from evil.
For thine is the kingdom,
   and the power,
   and the glory, forever. Amen.

CLOSING

Leader: Let us bless the Lord for this graduation day.
People: **Thanks be to God.**

A Liturgy for Baptism

OPENING

Leader: There is one body and one Spirit.
People: **One Lord, one faith, one baptism.**

SCRIPTURE

"Therefore go and make disciples of all nations, baptizing them in the name of the Father and of the Son and of the Holy Spirit, and teaching them to obey everything I have commanded you. And surely I am with you always, to the very end of the age." (Matt. 28:19-20)

Leader: The Word of the Lord.
People: **Thanks be to God.**

PRAYER

Leader: The Lord be with you.
People: **And also with you.**
Leader: Let us pray.

Heavenly Father, we thank you that by water and the Holy Spirit you have bestowed upon _____ (insert name) the forgiveness of sin, and have raised him/her to the new life of grace. Sustain him/her, O Lord, in your Holy Spirit. Give him/her the courage and will to persevere, a spirit to know and to love you, and the gift of joy and wonder in all your works. Amen.

REFLECTION

At this time, you may take a few minutes for a short reflection or personal prayer that goes along with the theme of the day.

THE LORD'S PRAYER

Our Father, who art in heaven,
   hallowed be thy name.
   thy kingdom come,

thy will be done
on earth as it is in heaven.
Give us this day our daily bread.
And forgive us our trespasses,
    as we forgive those who trespass against us.
And lead us not into temptation,
    but deliver us from evil.
For thine is the kingdom,
    and the power,
    and the glory, forever. Amen.

CLOSING

Leader: Let us bless the Lord for waters of baptism.
People: **Thanks be to God.**

A Liturgy for Confirmation

OPENING

Leader: The peace of the Lord be always with you.
People: **And with your spirit.**

SCRIPTURE

"Be strong and very courageous. Be careful to obey all the law my servant Moses gave you; do not turn from it to the right or to the left, that you may be successful wherever you go. Keep this Book of the Law always on your lips; meditate on it day and night, so that you may be careful to do everything written in it. Then you will be prosperous and successful. Have I not commanded you? Be strong and courageous. Do not be afraid; do not be discouraged, for the Lord your God will be with you wherever you go." (Josh. 1:7–9)

Leader: The Word of the Lord.
People: **Thanks be to God.**

PRAYER

Leader: The Lord be with you.
People: **And also with you.**
Leader: Let us pray.

Almighty and ever-living God, let your fatherly hand ever be over your servant, _____ (insert name); let your Holy Spirit ever be with him/her; and so lead him/her in the knowledge and obedience of your Word, that they may serve you in this life and dwell with you in the life to come, through Jesus Christ our Lord. Amen.

REFLECTION

At this time, you may take a few minutes for a short reflection or personal prayer that goes along with the theme of the day.

THE LORD'S PRAYER

Our Father, who art in heaven,
   hallowed be thy name.
   thy kingdom come,
   thy will be done
   on earth as it is in heaven.
Give us this day our daily bread.
And forgive us our trespasses,
   as we forgive those who trespass against us.
And lead us not into temptation,
   but deliver us from evil.
For thine is the kingdom,
   and the power,
   and the glory, forever. Amen.

CLOSING

Leader: Let us bless the Lord for the gift of the Holy Spirit.
People: **Thanks be to God.**

A Liturgy in Celebration of Diversity

OPENING

Leader: There is neither Jew nor Greek, there is neither slave nor free.
People: **For we are all one in Christ Jesus.**

SCRIPTURE

After this I looked, and there before me was a great multitude that no one could count, from every nation, tribe, people and language, standing before the throne and before the Lamb. They were wearing white robes and were holding palm branches in their hands. (Rev. 7:9)

Leader: The Word of the Lord.
People: **Thanks be to God.**

PRAYER

Leader: The Lord be with you.
People: **And also with you.**
Leader: Let us pray.

O God, who created all peoples in your image, we thank you for the wonderful diversity of races and cultures in this world. Enrich our lives by ever-widening circles of fellowship, and show us your presence in those who differ most from us, until our knowledge of your love is made perfect in our love for all your children, through Jesus Christ our Lord. Amen.

REFLECTION

At this time, you may take a few minutes for a short reflection or personal prayer that goes along with the theme of the day.

THE LORD'S PRAYER

Our Father, who art in heaven,
   hallowed be thy name.
   thy kingdom come,
   thy will be done
   on earth as it is in heaven.
Give us this day our daily bread.
And forgive us our trespasses,
   as we forgive those who trespass against us.
And lead us not into temptation,
   but deliver us from evil.
For thine is the kingdom,
   and the power,
   and the glory, forever. Amen.

CLOSING

Leader: Let us bless the Lord for the diversity of races and culture.
People: **Thanks be to God.**

A Liturgy for Planting a Tree

OPENING

Leader: We plant this tree for the glory of God.
People: **May it grow strong roots in the good earth.**

SCRIPTURE

I looked, and there before me stood a tree in the middle of the land. Its height was enormous. The tree grew large and strong and its top touched the sky; it was visible to the ends of the earth. Its leaves were beautiful, its fruit abundant, and on it was food for all. Under it the wild animals found shelter, and the birds lived in its branches; from it every creature was fed. (Dan. 4:10–12)

Leader: The Word of the Lord.
People: **Thanks be to God.**

PRAYER

Leader: The Lord be with you.
People: **And also with you.**
Leader: Let us pray.

Almighty God, Creator of heaven and earth, the work of your hands have created all living things, including the plants of the field, the birds of the air, the fish in the sea, and the animals of the land. Today, we ask you to bless the planting of this tree for the glory of God. May its roots grow deep in the soil of the good earth, may its leaves offer shade to those who are weary, may its branches be strong so that birds may make their nests in it, may its fruit provide food for your creatures, and may it always be a sign of your tender loving care for us and for all of your creation. Amen.

REFLECTION

At this time, you may take a few minutes for a short reflection or personal prayer that goes along with the theme of the day.

THE LORD'S PRAYER

Our Father, who art in heaven,
   hallowed be thy name.
   thy kingdom come,
   thy will be done
   on earth as it is in heaven.
Give us this day our daily bread.
And forgive us our trespasses,
   as we forgive those who trespass against us.
And lead us not into temptation,
   but deliver us from evil.
For thine is the kingdom,
   and the power,
   and the glory, forever. Amen.

CLOSING

Leader: Let us bless the Lord for this tree.
People: **Thanks be to God.**

A Liturgy for a Love Feast

DESCRIPTION

A Love Feast is a communal meal shared among Christians that recalls the Lord's Supper Jesus shared with his disciples. The name comes from the Greek word *agape*, which means "love." It originated in the early church and took place in homes. Although it is closely connected to the Lord's Supper, the services are different. The Lord's Supper requires ordained clergy; a Love Feast can take place in a home and a nonordained Christian may conduct it. The typical format of a Love Feast includes sharing a communal meal, reading scriptures, sharing personal testimonies, and singing songs to the Lord. Often there is a loaf of bread that is broken, then passed from hand to hand as each person breaks off a piece and shares a word of testimony or a prayer.

OPENING

Leader: Be completely humble and gentle.
People: **Be patient, bearing with one another in love.**

SCRIPTURE

They devoted themselves to the apostles' teaching and to fellowship, to the breaking of bread and to prayer. Everyone was filled with awe at the many wonders and signs performed by the apostles. All the believers were together and had everything in common. They sold property and possessions to give to anyone who had need. Every day they continued to meet together in the temple courts. They broke bread in their homes and ate together with glad and sincere hearts, praising God and enjoying the favor of all the people. And the Lord added to their number daily those who were being saved. (Acts 2:42–47)

Leader: The Word of the Lord.
People: **Thanks be to God.**

PRAYER

Leader: The Lord be with you.
People: **And also with you.**
Leader: Let us pray.

Be present at our table, Lord;
Be here and everywhere adored;
Thy creatures bless, and grant that we
May feast in paradise with thee.

We thank you, Lord, for this our food,
For life and health and every good;
By your own hand may we be fed;
Give us each day our daily bread.

We thank you, Lord, for this our good,
But more because of Jesus' blood;
Let manna to our souls be given,
The Bread of Life sent down from heaven.

REFLECTION

At this time, pass the bread or food to all who are gathered around the table and allow each person to share a word of testimony or a prayer of thanksgiving to the Lord. You may also add more scriptures or songs of praise.

THE LORD'S PRAYER

Our Father, who art in heaven,
    hallowed be thy name.
    thy kingdom come,
    thy will be done
    on earth as it is in heaven.
Give us this day our daily bread.
And forgive us our trespasses,
    as we forgive those who trespass against us.
And lead us not into temptation,
    but deliver us from evil.
For thine is the kingdom,
    and the power,
    and the glory, forever. Amen.

CLOSING

Leader: Let us bless the Lord for the love that we share.
People: **Thanks be to God.**

Part 4
For Difficult Seasons

A Liturgy for Spiritual Warfare

OPENING

Leader: Submit yourselves to God.
People: **Resist the devil, and he will flee from you.**

SCRIPTURE

Put on the full armor of God, so that you can take your stand against the devil's schemes. For our struggle is not against flesh and blood, but against the rulers, against the authorities, against the powers of this dark world and against the spiritual forces of evil in the heavenly realms. Therefore put on the full armor of God, so that when the day of evil comes, you may be able to stand your ground, and after you have done everything, to stand. Stand firm then, with the belt of truth buckled around your waist, with the breastplate of righteousness in place, and with your feet fitted with the readiness that comes from the gospel of peace. In addition to all this, take up the shield of faith, with which you can extinguish all the flaming arrows of the evil one. Take the helmet of salvation and the sword of the Spirit, which is the word of God. (Eph. 6:11-17)

Leader: The Word of the Lord.
People: **Thanks be to God.**

PRAYER

Leader: The Lord be with you.
People: **And also with you.**
Leader: Let us pray.

Almighty God, you have called us to live as salt and light in a dark world and to stand against the works of darkness. In seasons when we encounter spiritual warfare, obstacles, and attacks of the enemy, arm us with the sword of the Spirit, the Word of God, to stand against the enemy's lies. Equip us with strength, wisdom, and discernment through the power of the Holy Spirit and send your angels to watch over us. Finally, remind us that you will never leave us nor forsake us in whatever battle we may face. All this we ask, in the powerful name of Jesus Christ, amen.

THE LORD'S PRAYER

Our Father, who art in heaven,
    hallowed be thy name.
    thy kingdom come,
    thy will be done
    on earth as it is in heaven.
Give us this day our daily bread.
And forgive us our trespasses,
    as we forgive those who trespass against us.
And lead us not into temptation,
    but deliver us from evil.
For thine is the kingdom,
    and the power,
    and the glory, forever. Amen.

REFLECTION

At this time, you may take a few minutes for a short reflection or personal prayer that goes along with the theme of the day.

CLOSING

Leader: Let us bless the Lord who fights our battles for us.
People: **Thanks be to God.**

A Liturgy for Overcoming Fear

OPENING

Leader: God has not given us a spirit of fear.
People: **But love, power, and sound mind.**

SCRIPTURE

But now, this is what the Lord says—
  he who created you, Jacob,
  he who formed you, Israel:
"Do not fear, for I have redeemed you;
  I have summoned you by name; you are mine.
When you pass through the waters,
  I will be with you;
and when you pass through the rivers,
  they will not sweep over you.
When you walk through the fire,
  you will not be burned;
  the flames will not set you ablaze." (Isa. 43:1–2)

Leader: The Word of the Lord.
People: **Thanks be to God.**

PRAYER

Leader: The Lord be with you.
People: **And also with you.**
Leader: Let us pray.

Most loving Father, you will us to give thanks for all things, to dread nothing but the loss of you, and to cast all our cares on the one who cares for us. Preserve us from faithless fears and worldly anxieties, and grant that no clouds of this mortal life may hide from us the light of that love which is immortal, and which you have manifested unto us in your Son, Jesus Christ our Lord. Amen.

REFLECTION

At this time, you may take a few minutes for a short reflection or personal prayer that goes along with the theme of the day.

THE LORD'S PRAYER

Our Father, who art in heaven,
    hallowed be thy name.
    thy kingdom come,
    thy will be done
    on earth as it is in heaven.
Give us this day our daily bread.
And forgive us our trespasses,
    as we forgive those who trespass against us.
And lead us not into temptation,
    but deliver us from evil.
For thine is the kingdom,
    and the power,
    and the glory, forever. Amen.

CLOSING

Leader: Let us bless the Lord who calms all our fears.
People: **Thanks be to God.**

A Liturgy for Things You Cannot Change

OPENING

Leader: Do not worry about tomorrow.
People: For tomorrow will take care of itself.

SCRIPTURE

"Therefore I tell you, do not worry about your life, what you will eat or drink; or about your body, what you will wear. Is not life more than food, and the body more than clothes? Look at the birds of the air; they do not sow or reap or store away in barns, and yet your heavenly Father feeds them. Are you not much more valuable than they? Can any one of you by worrying add a single hour to your life? . . . But seek first his kingdom and his righteousness, and all these things will be given to you as well. Therefore do not worry about tomorrow, for tomorrow will worry about itself. Each day has enough trouble of its own." (Matt. 6:25-27, 33-34)

Leader: The Word of the Lord.
People: Thanks be to God.

PRAYER

Leader: The Lord be with you.
People: And also with you.
Leader: Let us pray.

God, grant me the serenity
to accept the things I cannot change,
the courage to change the things I can,
and the wisdom to know the difference.
Living one day at a time,
enjoying one moment at a time;
accepting hardship as a pathway to peace;
taking, as Jesus did,
this sinful world as it is,

not as I would have it;
trusting that you will make all things right
if I surrender to your will;
so that I may be reasonably happy in this life
and supremely happy with you forever in the next.
Amen.

REFLECTION

At this time, you may take a few minutes for a short reflection or personal prayer that goes along with the theme of the day.

THE LORD'S PRAYER

Our Father, who art in heaven,
    hallowed be thy name.
    thy kingdom come,
    thy will be done
    on earth as it is in heaven.
Give us this day our daily bread.
And forgive us our trespasses,
    as we forgive those who trespass against us.
And lead us not into temptation,
    but deliver us from evil.
For thine is the kingdom,
    and the power,
    and the glory, forever. Amen.

CLOSING

Leader: Let us bless the Lord who gives us serenity.
People: Thanks be to God.

A Liturgy for Those Who Mourn

OPENING

Leader: There will be no more death, mourning, or crying or pain.
People: **I am making everything new!**

SCRIPTURE

Then I saw "a new heaven and a new earth," for the first heaven and the first earth had passed away, and there was no longer any sea. I saw the Holy City, the new Jerusalem, coming down out of heaven from God, prepared as a bride beautifully dressed for her husband. And I heard a loud voice from the throne saying, "Look! God's dwelling place is now among the people, and he will dwell with them. They will be his people, and God himself will be with them and be their God. 'He will wipe every tear from their eyes. There will be no more death' or mourning or crying or pain, for the old order of things has passed away."

He who was seated on the throne said, "I am making everything new!" Then he said, "Write this down, for these words are trustworthy and true." (Rev. 21:1-5)

Leader: The Word of the Lord.
People: **Thanks be to God.**

PRAYER

Leader: The Lord be with you.
People: **And also with you.**
Leader: Let us pray.

O God, who brought us to birth, and in whose arms we die, in our grief and shock contain and comfort us; embrace us with your love, give us hope in our confusion and grace to let go into new life. You have taught us in your holy Word that you do not willingly afflict or grieve your children. Look with pity on the sorrows of your children who mourn. Remember them, O Lord, in mercy; nourish our souls with patience; comfort us with a sense of your goodness; lift up your countenance upon us; and give us peace, through Jesus Christ our Lord. Amen.

REFLECTION

At this time, you may take a few minutes for a short reflection or personal prayer that goes along with the theme of the day.

THE LORD'S PRAYER

Our Father, who art in heaven,
   hallowed be thy name.
   thy kingdom come,
   thy will be done
   on earth as it is in heaven.
Give us this day our daily bread.
And forgive us our trespasses,
   as we forgive those who trespass against us.
And lead us not into temptation,
   but deliver us from evil.
For thine is the kingdom,
   and the power,
   and the glory, forever. Amen.

CLOSING

Leader: Let us bless the Lord for comforting those who mourn.
People: **Thanks be to God.**

A Liturgy for the Elderly

OPENING

Leader: Remember the days of old.
People: **Consider the generations past.**

SCRIPTURE

The righteous will flourish like a palm tree,
   they will grow like a cedar of Lebanon;
planted in the house of the Lord,
   they will flourish in the courts of our God.
They will still bear fruit in old age,
   they will stay fresh and green,
proclaiming, "The Lord is upright;
   he is my Rock, and there is no wickedness in him." (Ps. 92:12–15)

Leader: The Word of the Lord.
People: **Thanks be to God.**

PRAYER

Leader: The Lord be with you.
People: **And also with you.**
Leader: Let us pray.

Almighty God, your Word tells us that age is a gift and a sign of wisdom. Look with mercy, O God our Father, on all whose increasing years bring them weakness, distress, or isolation, especially _____ (insert name). Provide for them homes of dignity and peace; give them understanding helpers, and the willingness to accept help; and as their strength diminishes, increase their faith and their assurance of your love, through Jesus Christ our Lord. Amen.

REFLECTION

At this time, you may take a few minutes for a short reflection or personal prayer that goes along with the theme of the day.

THE LORD'S PRAYER

Our Father, who art in heaven,
   hallowed be thy name.
   thy kingdom come,
   thy will be done
   on earth as it is in heaven.
Give us this day our daily bread.
And forgive us our trespasses,
   as we forgive those who trespass against us.
And lead us not into temptation,
   but deliver us from evil.
For thine is the kingdom,
   and the power,
   and the glory, forever. Amen.

CLOSING

Leader: Let us bless the Lord for renewed strength and purpose for those in their advanced years.
People: **Thanks be to God.**

A Liturgy for Lament

OPENING

Leader: Out of the depths I cry to you, O Lord.
People: **Lord, hear my voice!**

SCRIPTURE

How long, Lord? Will you forget me forever?
   How long will you hide your face from me?
How long must I wrestle with my thoughts
   and day after day have sorrow in my heart?
   How long will my enemy triumph over me?

Look on me and answer, Lord my God.
   Give light to my eyes, or I will sleep in death,
and my enemy will say, "I have overcome him,"
   and my foes will rejoice when I fall.

But I trust in your unfailing love;
   my heart rejoices in your salvation.
I will sing the Lord's praise,
   for he has been good to me. (Ps. 13:1-6)

Leader: The Word of the Lord.
People: **Thanks be to God.**

PRAYER

Leader: The Lord be with you.
People: **And also with you.**
Leader: Let us pray.

Dear Jesus, you suffered pain, sorrow, and death. You invite us to bring our prayers of lament before you. We ask that you do not let us be put to shame, nor let our enemies triumph over us. Turn to us and be gracious to us, for we are lonely and afflicted in our sufferings. Relieve the troubles of our hearts and free us from our anguish. Look on our affliction and distress and take away all our sins. See how numerous are our enemies and how fiercely they hate us. We are overwhelmed and desperately need your intervention. Guard our lives and rescue us; do not let us be put to shame, for we take refuge in you. May integrity and uprightness protect us, because our hope, Lord, is in you. Amen.

REFLECTION

At this time, you may take a few minutes for a short reflection or personal prayer that goes along with the theme of the day.

THE LORD'S PRAYER

Our Father, who art in heaven,
   hallowed be thy name.
   thy kingdom come,
   thy will be done
   on earth as it is in heaven.
Give us this day our daily bread.
And forgive us our trespasses,
   as we forgive those who trespass against us.
And lead us not into temptation,
   but deliver us from evil.
For thine is the kingdom,
   and the power,
   and the glory, forever. Amen.

CLOSING

Leader: Let us bless the Lord who hears the cries of our hearts.
People: **Thanks be to God.**

A Liturgy for Justice and Peace

OPENING

Leader: What does the Lord require of you?
People: **To do justice, to love kindness, and to walk humbly with your God.**

SCRIPTURE

"The Spirit of the Lord is on me,
  because he has anointed me
  to proclaim good news to the poor.
He has sent me to proclaim freedom for the prisoners
  and recovery of sight for the blind,
to set the oppressed free,
  to proclaim the year of the Lord's favor." (Luke 4:18–19)

PRAYER

Leader: The Lord be with you.
People: **And also with you.**
Leader: Let us pray.

Grant, O God, that your Spirit may so move every human heart and especially the hearts of the people of this land, that barriers which divide us may crumble, suspicions disappear, and hatreds cease; that our divisions be healed, and that we may live together as one people. Help us, in the midst of our struggles for justice, equality, and truth, to confront one another without hatred or bitterness, and to work together with mutual forbearance and respect, that we may be one, through Jesus Christ our Lord. Amen.

REFLECTION

At this time, you may take a few minutes for a short reflection or personal prayer that goes along with the theme of the day.

THE LORD'S PRAYER

Our Father, who art in heaven,
   hallowed be thy name.
   thy kingdom come,
   thy will be done
   on earth as it is in heaven.
Give us this day our daily bread.
And forgive us our trespasses,
   as we forgive those who trespass against us.
And lead us not into temptation,
   but deliver us from evil.
For thine is the kingdom,
   and the power,
   and the glory, forever. Amen.

CLOSING

Leader: Let us bless the Lord who desires justice, equality, and truth.
People: **Thanks be to God.**

A Liturgy for the Loss of Work

OPENING

Leader: Fear not, for I am with you
People: Be not dismayed, for I am your God.

SCRIPTURE

The Lord makes firm the steps
   of the one who delights in him;
though he may stumble, he will not fall,
for the Lord upholds him with his hand.

I was young and now I am old,
   yet I have never seen the righteous forsaken
   or their children begging bread.
They are always generous and lend freely;
   their children will be a blessing. (Ps. 37:23-26)

Leader: The Word of the Lord.
People: Thanks be to God.

PRAYER

Leader: The Lord be with you.
People: And also with you.
Leader: Let us pray.

Almighty God, today I stand before you, having recently lost my job. I am struggling right now and having a hard time. Please shine your light down on me, Lord, and give me the guidance to get through this difficult season in my life. Give me the peace and assurance that you will continue to provide for me and my family during this difficult and uncertain time. Your Word tells us to fear not; therefore, I trust and believe that you will make a way. Let me know clearly what you are calling me to do in life and grant me every grace I need to answer your call with courage. Amen.

REFLECTION

At this time, you may take a few minutes for a short reflection or personal prayer that goes along with the theme of the day.

THE LORD'S PRAYER

Our Father, who art in heaven,
   hallowed be thy name.
   thy kingdom come,
   thy will be done
   on earth as it is in heaven.
Give us this day our daily bread.
And forgive us our trespasses,
   as we forgive those who trespass against us.
And lead us not into temptation,
   but deliver us from evil.
For thine is the kingdom,
   and the power,
   and the glory, forever. Amen.

CLOSING

Leader: Let us bless the Lord for help in difficult times.
People: **Thanks be to God.**

A Liturgy for the Depressed and Downcast

OPENING

Leader: May the God of hope fill you with all joy and peace.
People: **May you overflow with hope by the power of the Holy Spirit.**

SCRIPTURE

Why, my soul, are you downcast?
   Why so disturbed within me?
Put your hope in God,
   for I will yet praise him,
   my Savior and my God.

My soul is downcast within me;
   therefore I will remember you
from the land of the Jordan,
   the heights of Hermon—from Mount Mizar.
Deep calls to deep
   in the roar of your waterfalls;
all your waves and breakers
   have swept over me.

By day the Lord directs his love,
   at night his song is with me—
   a prayer to the God of my life. (Ps. 42:5–8)

Leader: The Word of the Lord.
People: **Thanks be to God.**

PRAYER

Leader: The Lord be with you.
People: **And also with you.**
Leader: Let us pray.

O God, almighty and merciful, you heal the brokenhearted, and turn the sadness of the sorrowful to joy. Let your fatherly goodness be upon all whom you have made. Remember in pity all those who are this day destitute, homeless, elderly, infirm, or forgotten. Bless the multitude of your poor. Lift up those who are cast down. Mightily befriend innocent sufferers, and sanctify to them the endurance of their wrongs. Cheer with hope all who are discouraged and downcast, and by your heavenly grace preserve from falling those whose poverty tempts them to sin. Though they be troubled on every side, suffer them not to be distressed; though they are perplexed, save them from despair. Grant this, O Lord, for the love of him who for our sakes became poor, your Son our Savior Jesus Christ. Amen.

REFLECTION

At this time, you may take a few minutes for a short reflection or personal prayer that goes along with the theme of the day.

THE LORD'S PRAYER

Our Father, who art in heaven,
    hallowed be thy name.
    thy kingdom come,
    thy will be done
    on earth as it is in heaven.
Give us this day our daily bread.
And forgive us our trespasses,
    as we forgive those who trespass against us.
And lead us not into temptation,
    but deliver us from evil.
For thine is the kingdom,
    and the power,
    and the glory, forever. Amen.

CLOSING

Leader: Let us bless the Lord for bringing hope to the hopeless.
People: **Thanks be to God.**

A Liturgy for the Poor and the Neglected

OPENING

Leader: Blessed are you who are poor.
People: **For yours is the kingdom of God.**

SCRIPTURE

[Jesus] stood up to read, and the scroll of the prophet Isaiah was handed to him. Unrolling it, he found the place where it is written:
 "The Spirit of the Lord is on me,
  because he has anointed me
  to proclaim good news to the poor.
 He has sent me to proclaim freedom for the prisoners
  and recovery of sight for the blind,
 to set the oppressed free,
  to proclaim the year of the Lord's favor." (Luke 4:16b–19)

Leader: The Word of the Lord.
People: **Thanks be to God.**

PRAYER

Leader: The Lord be with you.
People: **And also with you.**
Leader: Let us pray.

Almighty and most merciful God, we remember before you all poor and neglected persons whom it would be easy for us to forget: the homeless and the destitute, the old and the sick, and all who have none to care for them. Help us to heal those who are broken in body or spirit, and to turn their sorrow into joy. Grant this, Father, for the love of your Son, who for our sake became poor, Jesus Christ our Lord. Amen.

REFLECTION

At this time, you may take a few minutes for a short reflection or personal prayer that goes along with the theme of the day.

THE LORD'S PRAYER

Our Father, who art in heaven,
   hallowed be thy name.
   thy kingdom come,
   thy will be done
   on earth as it is in heaven.
Give us this day our daily bread.
And forgive us our trespasses,
   as we forgive those who trespass against us.
And lead us not into temptation,
   but deliver us from evil.
For thine is the kingdom,
   and the power,
   and the glory, forever. Amen.

CLOSING

Leader: Let us bless the Lord who cares for the poor and neglected.
People: **Thanks be to God.**

A Liturgy for the Death of a Loved One

OPENING

Leader: Blessed are the dead who die in the Lord.
People: **For they rest from their labors.**

SCRIPTURE

"I am the resurrection and the life. The one who believes in me will live, even though they die; and whoever lives by believing in me will never die." (John 11:25-26)

Leader: The Word of the Lord.
People: **Thanks be to God.**

PRAYER

Leader: The Lord be with you.
People: **And also with you.**
Leader: Let us pray.

Almighty God, Father of mercies and giver of comfort: today we remember our loved one _____ (insert name), who has died and departed this world and has gone to be with you in the next. Surround us with your love, that we may not be overwhelmed by our loss, but have confidence in your goodness, and strength that we may remember and celebrate his/her life in the days to come. Deal graciously, we pray, with all of us who mourn; that, casting all our cares upon you, we may know the consolation of your love, through Jesus Christ our Lord. Amen.

REFLECTION

At this time, you may take a few minutes for a short reflection or personal prayer that goes along with the theme of the day.

THE LORD'S PRAYER

Our Father, who art in heaven,
   hallowed be thy name.
   thy kingdom come,
   thy will be done
   on earth as it is in heaven.
Give us this day our daily bread.
And forgive us our trespasses,
   as we forgive those who trespass against us.
And lead us not into temptation,
   but deliver us from evil.
For thine is the kingdom,
   and the power,
   and the glory, forever. Amen.

CLOSING

Leader: Let us bless the Lord for the memory of our loved one.
People: **Thanks be to God.**

A Liturgy for Those with Addiction

OPENING

Leader: Wherever the Spirit of the Lord is . . .
People: **There is liberty!**

SCRIPTURE

The Spirit of the Sovereign Lord is on me,
    because the Lord has anointed me
    to proclaim good news to the poor.
He has sent me to bind up the brokenhearted,
    to proclaim freedom for the captives
    and release from darkness for the prisoners,
to proclaim the year of the Lord's favor
    and the day of vengeance of our God,
to comfort all who mourn,
    and provide for those who grieve in Zion—
to bestow on them a crown of beauty
    instead of ashes,
the oil of joy
    instead of mourning,
and a garment of praise
    instead of a spirit of despair.
They will be called oaks of righteousness,
    a planting of the Lord
for the display of his splendor. (Isa. 61:1-3)

Leader: The Word of the Lord.
People: **Thanks be to God.**

PRAYER

Leader: The Lord be with you.
People: **And also with you.**
Leader: Let us pray.

O blessed Lord, you came to set the captives free and ministered to all who came to you. Look with compassion upon those who, through addiction, have lost their health and freedom. Restore to them the assurance of your unfailing mercy; remove from them the fears that beset them; strengthen them in the work of their recovery. And to those who minister to them, give patient understanding and persevering love, through Jesus Christ our Lord. Amen.

REFLECTION

At this time, you may take a few minutes for a short reflection or personal prayer that goes along with the theme of the day.

THE LORD'S PRAYER

Our Father, who art in heaven,
    hallowed be thy name.
    thy kingdom come,
    thy will be done
    on earth as it is in heaven.
Give us this day our daily bread.
And forgive us our trespasses,
    as we forgive those who trespass against us.
And lead us not into temptation,
    but deliver us from evil.
For thine is the kingdom,
    and the power,
    and the glory, forever. Amen.

CLOSING

Leader: Let us bless the Lord for setting the captives free!
People: **Thanks be to God.**

A Liturgy for God's Healing

OPENING

Leader: I will restore you to health.
People: **And heal your wounds.**

SCRIPTURE

Is anyone among you in trouble? Let them pray. Is anyone happy? Let them sing songs of praise. Is anyone among you sick? Let them call the elders of the church to pray over them and anoint them with oil in the name of the Lord. And the prayer offered in faith will make the sick person well; the Lord will raise them up. If they have sinned, they will be forgiven. Therefore confess your sins to each other and pray for each other so that you may be healed. The prayer of a righteous person is powerful and effective. (James 5:14–16)

Leader: The Word of the Lord.
People: **Thanks be to God.**

PRAYER

Leader: The Lord be with you.
People: **And also with you.**
Leader: Let us pray.

Almighty God, you are the source of all health and healing. Today we humbly pray that you would drive away from our bodies all sickness and infirmity. Please be present in your goodness with your servant _____ (insert name), that sickness may be healed and strength restored; and that, his/her health being renewed, he/she may bless your holy name, through Jesus Christ our Lord. Amen.

REFLECTION

At this time, you may take a few minutes for a short reflection or personal prayer that goes along with the theme of the day.

THE LORD'S PRAYER

Our Father, who art in heaven,
   hallowed be thy name.
   thy kingdom come,
   thy will be done
   on earth as it is in heaven.
Give us this day our daily bread.
And forgive us our trespasses,
   as we forgive those who trespass against us.
And lead us not into temptation,
   but deliver us from evil.
For thine is the kingdom,
   and the power,
   and the glory, forever. Amen.

CLOSING

Leader: Let us bless the Lord for the promise of healing.
People: **Thanks be to God.**

A Liturgy for Times of Trouble

OPENING

Leader:　God is our refuge and strength.
People:　**An ever-present help in trouble.**

SCRIPTURE

The Lord is my shepherd, I lack nothing.
　　He makes me lie down in green pastures,
he leads me beside quiet waters,
　　he refreshes my soul.
He guides me along the right paths
　　for his name's sake.
Even though I walk
　　through the darkest valley,
I will fear no evil,
　　for you are with me;
your rod and your staff,
　　they comfort me.

You prepare a table before me
　　in the presence of my enemies.
You anoint my head with oil;
　　my cup overflows.
Surely your goodness and love will follow me
　　all the days of my life,
and I will dwell in the house of the Lord
　　forever. (Ps. 23)

Leader:　The Word of the Lord.
People:　**Thanks be to God.**

PRAYER

Leader:　The Lord be with you.
People:　**And also with you.**
Leader:　Let us pray.

Dear Lord, you are the risen Christ, the Prince of Peace, the Mighty God, and the Everlasting Counselor. Grant us peace of mind and help our hearts to not be troubled during these difficult and uncertain times. Give us the strength and grace to trust you even when we cannot see the way. Remind us that you will never let us go and that you will always hold us in your everlasting arms of love. We ask all of this in the name of Jesus Christ our Lord, amen.

REFLECTION

At this time, you may take a few minutes for a short reflection or personal prayer that goes along with the theme of the day.

THE LORD'S PRAYER

Our Father, who art in heaven,
    hallowed be thy name.
    thy kingdom come,
    thy will be done
    on earth as it is in heaven.
Give us this day our daily bread.
And forgive us our trespasses,
    as we forgive those who trespass against us.
And lead us not into temptation,
    but deliver us from evil.
For thine is the kingdom,
    and the power,
    and the glory, forever. Amen.

CLOSING

Leader: Let us bless the Lord for comfort during the troubled times.
People: **Thanks be to God.**

A Liturgy for Times of Natural Disaster

OPENING

Leader: For the mountains may depart and the hills be removed.
People: **But my steadfast love shall not depart from you.**

SCRIPTURE

God is our refuge and strength,
 an ever-present help in trouble.
Therefore we will not fear, though the earth give way
 and the mountains fall into the heart of the sea,
though its waters roar and foam
 and the mountains quake with their surging.

There is a river whose streams make glad the city of God,
 the holy place where the Most High dwells.
God is within her, she will not fall;
 God will help her at break of day.
Nations are in uproar, kingdoms fall;
 he lifts his voice, the earth melts.

The Lord Almighty is with us;
 the God of Jacob is our fortress. (Ps. 46:1–7)

Leader: The Word of the Lord.
People: **Thanks be to God.**

PRAYER

Leader: The Lord be with you.
People: **And also with you.**
Leader: Let us pray.

Almighty God, by your Word you laid the foundations of the earth, set the bounds of the sea, and still the wind and waves. Surround us with your grace and peace, and preserve us through this storm (or _____). By your Spirit, lift up those who have fallen, strengthen those who work to rescue or rebuild, and fill us with the hope of your new creation, through Jesus Christ our Lord. Amen.

REFLECTION

At this time, you may take a few minutes for a short reflection or personal prayer that goes along with the theme of the day.

THE LORD'S PRAYER

Our Father, who art in heaven,
   hallowed be thy name.
   thy kingdom come,
   thy will be done
   on earth as it is in heaven.
Give us this day our daily bread.
And forgive us our trespasses,
   as we forgive those who trespass against us.
And lead us not into temptation,
   but deliver us from evil.
For thine is the kingdom,
   and the power,
   and the glory, forever. Amen.

CLOSING

Leader: Let us bless the Lord for protecting us from harm.
People: **Thanks be to God.**

A Liturgy for Social Conflict and Distress

OPENING

Leader: Rejoice in hope, be patient in tribulation.
People: **Be constant in prayer.**

SCRIPTURE

Whoever dwells in the shelter of the Most High
 will rest in the shadow of the Almighty.
I will say of the Lord, "He is my refuge and my fortress,
 my God, in whom I trust."

Surely he will save you
 from the fowler's snare
 and from the deadly pestilence.
He will cover you with his feathers,
 and under his wings you will find refuge;
 his faithfulness will be your shield and rampart.
You will not fear the terror of night,
 nor the arrow that flies by day,
nor the pestilence that stalks in the darkness,
 nor the plague that destroys at midday.
A thousand may fall at your side,
 ten thousand at your right hand,
 but it will not come near you. (Ps. 91:1–7)

Leader: The Word of the Lord.
People: **Thanks be to God.**

PRAYER

Leader: The Lord be with you.
People: **And also with you.**
Leader: Let us pray.

Increase, O God, the spirit of neighborliness among us, that in peril, we may uphold one another; in suffering, tend to one another; and in homelessness, loneliness, or exile, befriend one another. Grant us brave and enduring hearts, that we may strengthen one another until the disciplines and testing of these days are ended, and you again give peace in our time, through Jesus Christ our Lord. Amen.

REFLECTION

At this time, you may take a few minutes for a short reflection or personal prayer that goes along with the theme of the day.

THE LORD'S PRAYER

Our Father, who art in heaven,
   hallowed be thy name.
   thy kingdom come,
   thy will be done
   on earth as it is in heaven.
Give us this day our daily bread.
And forgive us our trespasses,
   as we forgive those who trespass against us.
And lead us not into temptation,
   but deliver us from evil.
For thine is the kingdom,
   and the power,
   and the glory, forever. Amen.

CLOSING

Leader: Let us bless the Lord for protecting us from harm.
People: **Thanks be to God.**

Part 5
For Holy Days and Holidays

A Liturgy for Advent

OPENING

Leader: Prepare the way for the Lord.
People: **Make straight in the desert a highway for our God.**

SCRIPTURE

The beginning of the good news about Jesus the Messiah, the Son of God, as it is written in Isaiah the prophet:
"I will send my messenger ahead of you,
 who will prepare your way"—
"a voice of one calling in the wilderness,
'Prepare the way for the Lord,
 make straight paths for him.'" (Mark 1:1-3)

Leader: The Word of the Lord.
People: **Thanks be to God.**

PRAYER

Leader: The Lord be with you.
People: **And also with you.**
Leader: Let us pray.

Merciful God, who sent your messengers, the prophets, to preach repentance and prepare the way for our salvation, give us grace to hear their warnings and turn from our sins, that we may greet with joy the coming of Jesus Christ our Redeemer, who lives and reigns with you and the Holy Spirit, one God, now and forever. Amen.

REFLECTION

At this time, you may take a few minutes for a short reflection or personal prayer that goes along with the theme of the day.

THE LORD'S PRAYER

Our Father, who art in heaven,
   hallowed be thy name.
   thy kingdom come,
   thy will be done
   on earth as it is in heaven.
Give us this day our daily bread.
And forgive us our trespasses,
   as we forgive those who trespass against us.
And lead us not into temptation,
   but deliver us from evil.
For thine is the kingdom,
   and the power,
   and the glory, forever. Amen.

CLOSING

Leader: Let us bless the Lord for making a way in the desert.
People: **Thanks be to God.**

A Liturgy for Christmas

OPENING

Leader: For unto you is born this day in the city of David . . .
People: **A Savior, who is Christ our Lord.**

SCRIPTURE

So Joseph also went up from the town of Nazareth in Galilee to Judea, to Bethlehem the town of David, because he belonged to the house and line of David. He went there to register with Mary, who was pledged to be married to him and was expecting a child. While they were there, the time came for the baby to be born, and she gave birth to her firstborn, a son. She wrapped him in cloths and placed him in a manger, because there was no guest room available for them.

    And there were shepherds living out in the fields nearby, keeping watch over their flocks at night. An angel of the Lord appeared to them, and the glory of the Lord shone around them, and they were terrified. But the angel said to them, "Do not be afraid. I bring you good news that will cause great joy for all the people. Today in the town of David a Savior has been born to you; he is the Messiah, the Lord. This will be a sign to you: You will find a baby wrapped in cloths and lying in a manger." (Luke 2:4–12)

Leader: The Word of the Lord.
People: **Thanks be to God.**

PRAYER

Leader: The Lord be with you.
People: **And also with you.**
Leader: Let us pray.

O God, you make us glad by the yearly festival of the birth of your only Son, Jesus Christ. Grant that we, who joyfully receive him as our Redeemer, may with sure confidence behold him when he comes to be our Judge, who lives and reigns with you and the Holy Spirit, one God, now and forever. Amen.

LIVING ROOM LITURGY

REFLECTION

At this time, you may take a few minutes for a short reflection or personal prayer that goes along with the theme of the day.

THE LORD'S PRAYER

Our Father, who art in heaven,
   hallowed be thy name.
   thy kingdom come,
   thy will be done
   on earth as it is in heaven.
Give us this day our daily bread.
And forgive us our trespasses,
   as we forgive those who trespass against us.
And lead us not into temptation,
   but deliver us from evil.
For thine is the kingdom,
   and the power,
   and the glory, forever. Amen.

CLOSING

Leader: Let us bless the Lord for the birth of Jesus Christ!
People: **Thanks be to God.**

A Liturgy for Epiphany

OPENING

Leader: You will be a light to the Gentiles.

People: **And salvation unto the ends of the earth.**

SCRIPTURE

"My name will be great among the nations, from where the sun rises to where it sets. In every place incense and pure offerings will be brought to me, because my name will be great among the nations," says the Lord Almighty. (Mal. 1:11)

Leader: The Word of the Lord.

People: **Thanks be to God.**

PRAYER

Leader: The Lord be with you.

People: **And also with you.**

Leader: Let us pray.

O God, by the leading of a star you manifested your only Son to the peoples of the earth. Lead us, who know you now by faith, to your presence, where we may see your glory face-to-face, through Jesus Christ our Lord, who lives and reigns with you and the Holy Spirit, one God, now and forever. Amen.

REFLECTION

At this time, you may take a few minutes for a short reflection or personal prayer that goes along with the theme of the day.

THE LORD'S PRAYER

Our Father, who art in heaven,
   hallowed be thy name.
   thy kingdom come,
   thy will be done
   on earth as it is in heaven.

Give us this day our daily bread.
And forgive us our trespasses,
   as we forgive those who trespass against us.
And lead us not into temptation,
   but deliver us from evil.
For thine is the kingdom,
   and the power,
   and the glory, forever. Amen.

CLOSING

Leader: Let us bless the Lord for giving us the Light of the world.
People: **Thanks be to God.**

A Liturgy for Lent

OPENING

Leader: Rend your hearts and not your garments.
People: And turn to the Lord your God.

SCRIPTURE

If we claim to be without sin, we deceive ourselves and the truth is not in us. If we confess our sins, he is faithful and just and will forgive us our sins and purify us from all unrighteousness. (1 John 1:8–9)

Leader: The Word of the Lord.
People: Thanks be to God.

PRAYER

Leader: The Lord be with you.
People: And also with you.
Leader: Let us pray.

Almighty God, whose blessed Son was led by the Spirit to be tempted by Satan, come quickly to help us who are assaulted by many temptations. And, as you know the weaknesses of each of us, let each one find you mighty to save, through Jesus Christ your Son our Lord, who lives and reigns with you and the Holy Spirit, one God, now and forever. Amen.

REFLECTION

At this time, you may take a few minutes for a short reflection or personal prayer that goes along with the theme of the day.

THE LORD'S PRAYER

Our Father, who art in heaven,
   hallowed be thy name.
   thy kingdom come,
   thy will be done
   on earth as it is in heaven.

Give us this day our daily bread.
And forgive us our trespasses,
    as we forgive those who trespass against us.
And lead us not into temptation,
    but deliver us from evil.
For thine is the kingdom,
    and the power,
    and the glory, forever. Amen.

CLOSING

Leader: Let us bless the Lord for he forgives our sins.
People: **Thanks be to God.**

A Liturgy for Holy Week

OPENING

Leader: All we like sheep have gone astray; we have turned—every one—to his own way.
People: **The Lord has laid on him the iniquity of us all.**

SCRIPTURE

For God so loved the world that he gave his one and only Son, that whoever believes in him shall not perish but have eternal life. For God did not send his Son into the world to condemn the world, but to save the world through him. Whoever believes in him is not condemned, but whoever does not believe stands condemned already because they have not believed in the name of God's one and only Son. This is the verdict: Light has come into the world, but people loved darkness instead of light because their deeds were evil. Everyone who does evil hates the light, and will not come into the light for fear that their deeds will be exposed. But whoever lives by the truth comes into the light, so that it may be seen plainly that what they have done has been done in the sight of God. (John 3:16–21)

Leader: The Word of the Lord.
People: **Thanks be to God.**

PRAYER

Leader: The Lord be with you.
People: **And also with you.**
Leader: Let us pray.

Almighty God, we pray you graciously to behold this your family, for whom our Lord Jesus Christ was willing to be betrayed, and given into the hands of sinners, and to suffer death upon the cross, who now lives and reigns with you and the Holy Spirit, one God, forever and ever. Amen.

REFLECTION

At this time, you may take a few minutes for a short reflection or personal prayer that goes along with the theme of the day.

THE LORD'S PRAYER

Our Father, who art in heaven,
   hallowed be thy name.
   thy kingdom come,
   thy will be done
   on earth as it is in heaven.
Give us this day our daily bread.
And forgive us our trespasses,
   as we forgive those who trespass against us.
And lead us not into temptation,
   but deliver us from evil.
For thine is the kingdom,
   and the power,
   and the glory, forever. Amen.

CLOSING

Leader: Let us bless the Lord for so loving the world that he gave his only Son.
People: **Thanks be to God.**

A Liturgy for Easter

OPENING

Leader: Alleluia! Christ is risen!
People: **The Lord is risen indeed! Alleluia!**

SCRIPTURE

After the Sabbath, at dawn on the first day of the week, Mary Magdalene and the other Mary went to look at the tomb.

There was a violent earthquake, for an angel of the Lord came down from heaven and, going to the tomb, rolled back the stone and sat on it. His appearance was like lightning, and his clothes were white as snow. The guards were so afraid of him that they shook and became like dead men.

The angel said to the women, "Do not be afraid, for I know that you are looking for Jesus, who was crucified. He is not here; he has risen, just as he said. Come and see the place where he lay. Then go quickly and tell his disciples: 'He has risen from the dead and is going ahead of you into Galilee. There you will see him.' Now I have told you."

So the women hurried away from the tomb, afraid yet filled with joy, and ran to tell his disciples. Suddenly Jesus met them. "Greetings," he said. They came to him, clasped his feet and worshiped him. Then Jesus said to them, "Do not be afraid. Go and tell my brothers to go to Galilee; there they will see me." (Matt. 28:1–10)

Leader: The Word of the Lord.
People: **Thanks be to God.**

PRAYER

Leader: The Lord be with you.
People: **And also with you.**
Leader: Let us pray.

Almighty God, who through your only begotten Son Jesus Christ, overcame death and opened to us the gate of everlasting life, grant that we, who celebrate with joy the day of the Lord's resurrection, may, by your life-giving Spirit, be delivered from sin and raised from death, through Jesus

Christ our Lord, who lives and reigns with you and the Holy Spirit, one God, now and forever. Amen.

REFLECTION

At this time, you may take a few minutes for a short reflection or personal prayer that goes along with the theme of the day.

THE LORD'S PRAYER

Our Father, who art in heaven,
   hallowed be thy name.
   thy kingdom come,
   thy will be done
   on earth as it is in heaven.
Give us this day our daily bread.
And forgive us our trespasses,
   as we forgive those who trespass against us.
And lead us not into temptation,
   but deliver us from evil.
For thine is the kingdom,
   and the power,
   and the glory, forever. Amen.

CLOSING

Leader: Alleluia! Christ is risen!
People: **The Lord is risen indeed! Alleluia!**

A Liturgy for Pentecost

OPENING

Leader: You send forth your Spirit.
People: And renew the face of the earth.

SCRIPTURE

When the day of Pentecost came, they were all together in one place. Suddenly a sound like the blowing of a violent wind came from heaven and filled the whole house where they were sitting. They saw what seemed to be tongues of fire that separated and came to rest on each of them. All of them were filled with the Holy Spirit and began to speak in other tongues as the Spirit enabled them. (Acts 2:1–4)

Leader: The Word of the Lord.
People: Thanks be to God.

PRAYER

Leader: The Lord be with you.
People: And also with you.
Leader: Let us pray.

O God, who on this day taught the hearts of your faithful people by sending to them the light of your Holy Spirit, grant us by the same Spirit to have a right judgment in all things, and evermore to rejoice in his holy comfort, through Jesus Christ your Son our Lord, who lives and reigns with you, in the unity of the Holy Spirit, one God, forever and ever. Amen.

REFLECTION

At this time, you may take a few minutes for a short reflection or personal prayer that goes along with the theme of the day.

THE LORD'S PRAYER

Our Father, who art in heaven,
    hallowed be thy name.

thy kingdom come,
thy will be done
on earth as it is in heaven.
Give us this day our daily bread.
And forgive us our trespasses,
   as we forgive those who trespass against us.
And lead us not into temptation,
   but deliver us from evil.
For thine is the kingdom,
   and the power,
   and the glory, forever. Amen.

CLOSING

Leader: Let us bless the Lord for sending the Holy Spirit.
People: **Thanks be to God.**

A Liturgy for Thanksgiving

OPENING

Leader: Let us give thanks to God our Father for all his gifts so freely given.
People: **We thank you, Lord.**

SCRIPTURE

Do not be anxious about anything, but in every situation, by prayer and petition, with thanksgiving, present your requests to God. And the peace of God, which transcends all understanding, will guard your hearts and your minds in Christ Jesus. (Phil. 4:6–7)

Leader: The Word of the Lord.
People: **Thanks be to God.**

PRAYER

Leader: The Lord be with you.
People: **And also with you.**
Leader: Let us pray.

Accept, O Lord, our thanks and praise for all that you have done for us. We thank you for the splendor of the whole creation, for the beauty of this world, for the wonder of life, and for the mystery of love. We thank you for the blessing of family and friends, and for the loving care that surrounds us on every side. We thank you for setting us at tasks that demand our best efforts, and for leading us to accomplishments that satisfy and delight us. We thank you also for those disappointments and failures that lead us to acknowledge our dependence on you alone. Above all, we thank you for your Son Jesus Christ; for the truth of his Word and the example of his life; for his steadfast obedience, by which he overcame temptation; for his dying, through which he conquered death; and for his rising to life again, in which we are raised to the life of your kingdom. Grant us the gift of your Spirit, that we may know Christ and make him known; and through him, at all times and in all places, may we give thanks to you in all things. Amen.

LIVING ROOM LITURGY

REFLECTION

At this time, you may take a few minutes for a short reflection or personal prayer that goes along with the theme of the day.

THE LORD'S PRAYER

Our Father, who art in heaven,
   hallowed be thy name.
   thy kingdom come,
   thy will be done
   on earth as it is in heaven.
Give us this day our daily bread.
And forgive us our trespasses,
   as we forgive those who trespass against us.
And lead us not into temptation,
   but deliver us from evil.
For thine is the kingdom,
   and the power,
   and the glory, forever. Amen.

CLOSING

Leader: Let us bless the Lord for all that he has done for us.
People: **Thanks be to God.**

A Liturgy for New Year

OPENING

Leader: This is the day that the Lord has made.
People: **We will rejoice and be glad in it.**

SCRIPTURE

"For I know the plans I have for you," declares the Lord, "plans to prosper you and not to harm you, plans to give you hope and a future. Then you will call on me and come and pray to me, and I will listen to you. You will seek me and find me when you seek me with all your heart." (Jer. 29:11–13)

Leader: The Word of the Lord.
People: **Thanks be to God.**

PRAYER

Leader: The Lord be with you.
People: **And also with you.**
Leader: Let us pray.

I am no longer my own, but thine. Put me to what thou wilt, rank me with whom thou wilt. Put me to doing, put me to suffering. Let me be employed by thee or laid aside for thee, exalted for thee or brought low for thee. Let me be full, let me be empty. Let me have all things, let me have nothing. I freely and heartily yield all things to thy pleasure and disposal. And now, O glorious and blessed God, Father, Son, and Holy Spirit, thou art mine, and I am thine. So be it. And the covenant which I have made on earth, let it be ratified in heaven. Amen. *(John Wesley's Covenant Prayer)*

REFLECTION

At this time, you may take a few minutes for a short reflection or personal prayer that goes along with the theme of the day.

THE LORD'S PRAYER

Our Father, who art in heaven,
   hallowed be thy name.
   thy kingdom come,
   thy will be done
   on earth as it is in heaven.
Give us this day our daily bread.
And forgive us our trespasses,
   as we forgive those who trespass against us.
And lead us not into temptation,
   but deliver us from evil.
For thine is the kingdom,
   and the power,
   and the glory, forever. Amen.

CLOSING

Leader: Let us bless the Lord for the beginning of a new year.
People: **Thanks be to God.**

A Liturgy for All Saints' Day

OPENING

Leader: To those sanctified in Christ Jesus.

People: **Called to be saints, together with all who call upon the name of our Lord.**

SCRIPTURE

Then I saw "a new heaven and a new earth," for the first heaven and the first earth had passed away, and there was no longer any sea. I saw the Holy City, the new Jerusalem, coming down out of heaven from God, prepared as a bride beautifully dressed for her husband. And I heard a loud voice from the throne saying, "Look! God's dwelling place is now among the people, and he will dwell with them. They will be his people, and God himself will be with them and be their God. 'He will wipe every tear from their eyes. There will be no more death' or mourning or crying or pain, for the old order of things has passed away."

He who was seated on the throne said, "I am making everything new!" Then he said, "Write this down, for these words are trustworthy and true."

He said to me: "It is done. I am the Alpha and the Omega, the Beginning and the End. To the thirsty I will give water without cost from the spring of the water of life." (Rev. 21:1-6)

Leader: The Word of the Lord.

People: **Thanks be to God.**

PRAYER

Leader: The Lord be with you.

People: **And also with you.**

Leader: Let us pray.

Almighty God, you have knit together your elect in one communion and fellowship in the mystical body of your Son, Christ our Lord. Give us grace so to follow your blessed saints in all virtuous and godly living, that we may come to those ineffable joys that you have prepared for those who truly love you, through Jesus Christ our Lord, who with you and the Holy Spirit lives and reigns, one God, in glory everlasting. Amen.

REFLECTION

At this time, you may take a few minutes for a short reflection or personal prayer that goes along with the theme of the day.

THE LORD'S PRAYER

Our Father, who art in heaven,
    hallowed be thy name.
    thy kingdom come,
    thy will be done
    on earth as it is in heaven.
Give us this day our daily bread.
And forgive us our trespasses,
    as we forgive those who trespass against us.
And lead us not into temptation,
    but deliver us from evil.
For thine is the kingdom,
    and the power,
    and the glory, forever. Amen.

CLOSING

Leader: Let us bless the Lord for all of the saints in heaven and earth.
People: **Thanks be to God.**

A Liturgy for St. Patrick's Day

OPENING

Leader: Therefore go and make disciples of all nations.
People: **Baptizing them in the name of the Father, the Son, and the Holy Spirit.**

SCRIPTURE

So Christ himself gave the apostles, the prophets, the evangelists, the pastors and teachers, to equip his people for works of service, so that the body of Christ may be built up until we all reach unity in the faith and in the knowledge of the Son of God and become mature, attaining to the whole measure of the fullness of Christ.

Then we will no longer be infants, tossed back and forth by the waves, and blown here and there by every wind of teaching and by the cunning and craftiness of people in their deceitful scheming. Instead, speaking the truth in love, we will grow to become in every respect the mature body of him who is the head, that is, Christ. From him the whole body, joined and held together by every supporting ligament, grows and builds itself up in love, as each part does its work. (Eph. 4:11–16)

Leader: The Word of the Lord.
People: **Thanks be to God.**

PRAYER

Leader: The Lord be with you.
People: **And also with you.**
Leader: Let us pray.

Almighty God, in your providence you chose your servant Patrick to be the apostle of the Irish people, to bring those who were wandering in darkness and error to the true light and knowledge of you. Grant us so to walk in that light that we may come at last to the light of everlasting life, through Jesus Christ our Lord, who lives and reigns with you and the Holy Spirit, one God, forever and ever. Amen.

LIVING ROOM LITURGY

REFLECTION

At this time, you may take a few minutes for a short reflection or personal prayer that goes along with the theme of the day.

THE LORD'S PRAYER

Our Father, who art in heaven,
   hallowed be thy name.
   thy kingdom come,
   thy will be done
   on earth as it is in heaven.
Give us this day our daily bread.
And forgive us our trespasses,
   as we forgive those who trespass against us.
And lead us not into temptation,
   but deliver us from evil.
For thine is the kingdom,
   and the power,
   and the glory, forever. Amen.

CLOSING

Leader: Let us bless the Lord for his servant, Saint Patrick.
People: **Thanks be to God.**

A Liturgy for the Advent Wreath

DESCRIPTION

The Advent wreath is rich in symbolism and represents the Christmas story. It is typically an evergreen wreath that contains five candles: three purple, one pink, and one white. The circle of greenery reminds us that God is eternal, the Alpha and Omega, without beginning or end. The candles symbolize the light of God entering the world through the birth of Jesus. The four outer candles represent a period of waiting for the birth of Jesus and their light reminds us that Jesus is the Light that comes into the darkness of our world. They also remind us that we are called to be a light as we reflect the light of God's love and grace to others.

The themes most often used for the four weeks of Advent are Hope, Peace, Joy, and Love. However, the choice of themes is not limited exclusively to these. The candles have different colors that remind us of the themes for Advent. Traditionally, the primary color of Lent is purple, which reflects fasting that formed part of the buildup to Christmas in earlier centuries. The color purple is also used at Advent to remind us of the link between the birth and death of Jesus. On the third Sunday of Advent, the color changes to pink, or rose, in anticipation of the birth of Jesus Christ. The center candle is white and is called the Christ Candle. It is traditionally lit on Christmas Eve or Christmas Day.

Over the Advent season, you can gather somewhere specific in your home and light a candle, read a portion of Scripture, and say a prayer each Sunday. Here is a list of prayers and verses to go with each theme as you use the Advent wreath.

FIRST SUNDAY: HOPE

The people walking in darkness
   have seen a great light;
on those living in the land of deep darkness
   a light has dawned. (Isa. 9:2)

One purple candle is lit.

Almighty God, as the Advent season begins, we cry out to you in hope because we live in a world of darkness and death. Loving God, remind us that our hope is in you. Wherever we find ourselves this season, be with us on this Advent journey. Amen.

SECOND SUNDAY: PEACE

For to us a child is born,
    to us a son is given,
        and the government will be on his shoulders.
And he will be called
    Wonderful Counselor, Mighty God,
    Everlasting Father, Prince of Peace.
Of the greatness of his government and peace
    there will be no end.
He will reign on David's throne
    and over his kingdom,
establishing and upholding it
    with justice and righteousness
    from that time on and forever.
The zeal of the Lord Almighty
    will accomplish this. (Isa. 9:6–7)

Two purple candles are lit.

Dear Jesus Christ, we pray that you would reveal yourself to us today as the Prince of Peace. You calm the wind and the waves. We need your peace in our lives, our homes, our families, our church, and our whole world. Help us to slow down and seek out the peace that only comes from you. As we receive your peace, make us peacemakers for others. Amen.

THIRD SUNDAY: JOY

But be glad and rejoice forever
    in what I will create,
for I will create Jerusalem to be a delight
    and its people a joy. (Isa. 65:18)

Two purple candles and one pink candle are lit.

FOR HOLY DAYS AND HOLIDAYS

Dear Jesus, only in you can we find joy. Help us to not to look to the things of this world for joy and fulfillment, but may we always look for the joy that comes from you and your kingdom. This week in our Advent journey, open our eyes to the joy that surrounds us. Amen.

FOURTH SUNDAY: LOVE

"A new command I give you: Love one another. As I have loved you, so you must love one another. By this everyone will know that you are my disciples, if you love one another." (John 13:34–35)

Three purple candles and one pink candle are lit.

Almighty and ever-living God, you loved us so much that you sent your only Son Jesus Christ to live and die for us. Today, we pray that you remind us of your love for us, that we may love one another and share your love with the world around us. May we always live in the reality of your free and eternal love for us. Amen.

CHRISTMAS DAY

While they were there, the time came for the baby to be born, and she gave birth to her firstborn, a son. She wrapped him in cloths and placed him in a manger, because there was no guest room available for them.

And there were shepherds living out in the fields nearby, keeping watch over their flocks at night. An angel of the Lord appeared to them, and the glory of the Lord shone around them, and they were terrified. But the angel said to them, "Do not be afraid. I bring you good news that will cause great joy for all the people. Today in the town of David a Savior has been born to you; he is the Messiah, the Lord." (Luke 2:6–11)

All five candles are lit.

Dear Jesus Christ, Son of God, we have been waiting all season for this most holy day of the year. On this Christmas Day, we celebrate that you were born in a humble manger to live and die as one of us. We pray that you would help us live as those who let hope, peace, joy, and love reign in our lives, our families, our home, and our world. As the candles burn brightly and light our home, let us live as those who have your light burning inside us today and each and every day. Amen.

Part 6
Calls and Responses

The Beatitudes

Leader: Blessed are the poor in spirit,
People: **for theirs is the kingdom of heaven.**

Leader: Blessed are those who mourn,
People: **for they will be comforted.**

Leader: Blessed are the meek,
People: **for they will inherit the earth.**

Leader: Blessed are those who hunger and thirst for righteousness,
People: **for they will be filled.**

Leader: Blessed are the merciful,
People: **for they will be shown mercy.**

Leader: Blessed are the pure in heart,
People: **for they will see God.**

Leader: Blessed are the peacemakers,
People: **for they will be called children of God.**

Leader: Blessed are those who are persecuted because of righteousness,
People: **for theirs is the kingdom of heaven.**

Leader: Blessed are you when people insult you, persecute you, and falsely say all kinds of evil against you because of me.
People: **Rejoice and be glad, because great is your reward in heaven, for in the same way they persecuted the prophets who were before you.**

A General Intercession

Leader: For the peace from above, for the lovingkindness of God, and for the salvation of our souls, let us pray to the Lord.
People: **Lord, have mercy.**

Leader: For the peace of the world, for the welfare of the holy church of God, and for the unity of all peoples, let us pray to the Lord.
People: **Lord, have mercy.**

Leader: For all the clergy and people, let us pray to the Lord.
People: **Lord, have mercy.**

Leader: For our president, for the leaders of the nations, and for all in authority, let us pray to the Lord.
People: **Lord, have mercy.**

Leader: For this city (town, village, etc.), for every city and community, and for those who live in them, let us pray to the Lord.
People: **Lord, have mercy.**

Leader: For seasonable weather, and for an abundance of the fruits of the earth, let us pray to the Lord.
People: **Lord, have mercy.**

Leader: For the good earth which God has given us, and for the wisdom and will to conserve it, let us pray to the Lord.
People: **Lord, have mercy.**

Leader: For those who travel on land, on water, or in the air (or through outer space), let us pray to the Lord.
People: **Lord, have mercy.**

Leader: For the aged and infirm, for the widowed and orphaned, and for the sick and the suffering, let us pray to the Lord.
People: **Lord, have mercy.**

Leader: For _____, let us pray to the Lord.
People: **Lord, have mercy.**

Leader:	For the poor and the oppressed, for the unemployed and the destitute, for prisoners and captives, and for all who remember and care for them, let us pray to the Lord.
People:	**Lord, have mercy.**
Leader:	For all who have died in the hope of the resurrection, and for all the departed, let us pray to the Lord.
People:	**Lord, have mercy.**
Leader:	For deliverance from all danger, violence, oppression, and degradation, let us pray to the Lord.
People:	**Lord, have mercy.**
Leader:	For the absolution and remission of our sins and offenses, let us pray to the Lord.
People:	**Lord, have mercy.**
Leader:	That we may end our lives in faith and hope, without suffering and without reproach, let us pray to the Lord.
People:	**Lord, have mercy.**
Leader:	Defend us, deliver us, and in thy compassion, protect us, O Lord, by thy grace.
People:	**Lord, have mercy.**
Leader:	In the communion of (_____ and of all the) saints, let us commend ourselves, and one another, and all our lives, to Christ our God.
People:	**To thee, O Lord our God.**

Affirming the Faith

Leader: Do you believe and trust in God the Father?
People: **I believe in God the Father Almighty, creator of heaven and earth.**

Leader: Do you believe and trust in Jesus Christ?
People: **I believe in Jesus Christ, his only Son, our Lord. He was conceived by the Holy Spirit and born of the Virgin Mary. He suffered under Pontius Pilate, was crucified, died, and was buried. He descended to the dead. On the third day he rose again. He ascended into heaven, and is seated at the right hand of the Father. He will come again to judge the living and the dead.**

Leader: Do you believe and trust in the Holy Spirit?
People: **I believe in the Holy Spirit,**
the holy Catholic church,
the communion of saints,
the forgiveness of sins,
the resurrection of the body,
and the life everlasting. Amen.

Leader: Let us pray.
Almighty God, you have built your church upon the foundation of the apostles and prophets, Jesus Christ himself being the chief cornerstone. Grant us so to be joined together in unity of spirit by their doctrine, that we may be made a holy temple acceptable to you, through Jesus Christ our Lord, who lives and reigns with you and the Holy Spirit, one God, world without end. Amen.

For Thanksgiving

Leader: Let us give thanks to God our Father for all his gifts so freely bestowed upon us,
People: **We thank you, Lord.**

Leader: For the beauty and wonder of your creation, in earth and sky and sea,
People: **We thank you, Lord.**

Leader: For all that is gracious in the lives of men and women, revealing the image of Christ,
People: **We thank you, Lord.**

Leader: For our daily food and drink, our homes and families, and our friends,
People: **We thank you, Lord.**

Leader: For minds to think, and hearts to love, and hands to serve,
People: **We thank you, Lord.**

Leader: For health and strength to work, and leisure to rest and play,
People: **We thank you, Lord.**

Leader: For the brave and courageous, who are patient in suffering and faithful in adversity,
People: **We thank you, Lord.**

Leader: For all valiant seekers after truth, liberty, and justice,
People: **We thank you, Lord.**

Leader: For the communion of saints, in all times and places,
People: **We thank you, Lord.**

Leader: Above all, we give you thanks for the great mercies and promises given to us in Christ Jesus our Lord.
People: **To him be praise and glory, with you, O Father, and the Holy Spirit, now and forever. Amen.**

For God's Deliverance

Leader: O God the Father, Creator of heaven and earth,
People: **Have mercy upon us.**

Leader: O God the Son, Redeemer of the world,
People: **Have mercy upon us.**

Leader: O God the Holy Spirit, Sanctifier of the faithful,
People: **Have mercy upon us.**

Leader: O holy, blessed, and glorious Trinity, one God,
People: **Have mercy upon us.**

Leader: Remember not, Lord Christ, our offenses, nor the offenses of our forefathers; neither reward us according to our sins. Spare us, good Lord, spare thy people, whom thou hast redeemed with thy most precious blood, and by thy mercy preserve us, forever.
People: **Spare us, good Lord.**

Leader: From all evil and wickedness; from sin; from the crafts and assaults of the devil; and from everlasting damnation,
People: **Good Lord, deliver us.**

Leader: From all blindness of heart; from pride, vainglory, and hypocrisy; from envy, hatred, and malice; and from all want of charity,
People: **Good Lord, deliver us.**

Leader: From all inordinate and sinful affections; and from all the deceits of the world, the flesh, and the devil,
People: **Good Lord, deliver us.**

Leader: From all false doctrine, heresy, and schism; from hardness of heart, and contempt of thy Word and commandment,
People: **Good Lord, deliver us.**

Leader: From lightning and tempest; from earthquake, fire, and flood; from plague, pestilence, and famine,
People: **Good Lord, deliver us.**

Leader: From all oppression, conspiracy, and rebellion; from violence, battle, and murder; and from dying suddenly and unprepared,
People: Good Lord, deliver us.

Leader: By the mystery of thy holy incarnation; by thy holy nativity and submission to the Law; by thy baptism, fasting, and temptation,
People: Good Lord, deliver us.

Leader: By thine agony and bloody sweat; by thy cross and passion; by thy precious death and burial; by thy glorious resurrection and ascension; and by the coming of the Holy Ghost,
People: Good Lord, deliver us.

Leader: In all time of our tribulation, in all time of our prosperity, in the hour of death, and in the day of judgment,
People: Good Lord, deliver us.

For the Beginning of Lent

OPENING

Leader: Bless the Lord who forgives all our sins.
People: **His mercy endures forever.**

The leader invites the people to the observance of a holy Lent, either here or following the sermon, saying:

Dear people of God, the first Christians observed with great devotion the days of our Lord's passion and resurrection, and it became the custom of the church to prepare for them by a season of penitence and fasting. This season of Lent provided a time in which converts to the faith were prepared for holy baptism. It was also a time when those who, because of notorious sins, had been separated from the body of the faithful, were reconciled by penitence and forgiveness, and restored to the fellowship of the church. In this manner, the whole congregation was put in mind of the message of pardon and absolution set forth in the gospel of our Savior, and of the need that all Christians continually have to renew our repentance and faith.

Let us humbly confess our sins to Almighty God.

Silence may follow. The leader and people, all kneeling, pray together:

Most holy and merciful Father,
we confess to you, and to one another,
and to the whole communion of saints
in heaven and on earth,
that we have sinned, through our own fault,
in thought, word, and deed,
by what we have done, and by what we have left undone.
We have not loved you with our whole heart, and mind, and strength.
We have not loved our neighbors as ourselves.
We have not forgiven others, as we have been forgiven.
We have been deaf to your call to serve, as Christ served us.
We have not been true to the mind of Christ.
We have grieved your Holy Spirit.

CALLS AND RESPONSES

Leader: Lord, have mercy upon us.
People: **For we have sinned against you.**

Leader: For all our unfaithfulness and disobedience; for the pride, vanity, and hypocrisy of our lives; Lord, have mercy upon us.
People: **For we have sinned against you.**

Leader: For our self-pity and impatience, and our envy of those we think more fortunate than ourselves; Lord, have mercy upon us.
People: **For we have sinned against you.**

Leader: For our unrighteous anger, bitterness, and resentment; for all lies, gossip, and slander against our neighbors; Lord, have mercy upon us.
People: **For we have sinned against you.**

Leader: For our sexual impurity, our exploitation of other people, and our failure to give of ourselves in love; Lord, have mercy upon us.
People: **For we have sinned against you.**

Leader: For our self-indulgent appetites and ways, and our intemperate pursuit of worldly goods and comforts; Lord, have mercy upon us.
People: **For we have sinned against you.**

Leader: For our dishonesty in daily life and work, our ingratitude for your gifts, and our failure to heed your call. Lord, have mercy upon us.
People: **For we have sinned against you.**

Leader: For our blindness to human need and suffering, and our indifference to injustice and cruelty; Lord, have mercy upon us.
People: **For we have sinned against you.**

Leader: For our wastefulness and misuse of your creation, and our lack of concern for those who come after us; Lord, have mercy upon us.
People: **For we have sinned against you.**

Leader: For all false judgments, for prejudice and contempt of others, and for all uncharitable thoughts toward our neighbors; Lord, have mercy upon us.
People: **For we have sinned against you.**

Leader: For our negligence in prayer and worship; for our presumption and abuse of your means of grace; Lord, have mercy upon us.
People: **For we have sinned against you.**

Leader: For seeking the praise of others rather than the approval of God; Lord, have mercy upon us.
People: **For we have sinned against you.**

Leader: For our failure to commend the faith that is in us; Lord, have mercy upon us.
People: **For we have sinned against you.**

The leader and people pray together:
Show favor to your people, O Lord, who turn to you in weeping, fasting, and prayer. For you are a merciful God, full of compassion, long-suffering, and abounding in steadfast love. You spare when we deserve punishment, and in your wrath you remember mercy. Spare your people, good Lord, spare us; in the multitude of your mercies, look upon us and forgive us, through the merits and mediation of your blessed Son Jesus Christ our Lord. Amen.

THE ABSOLUTION

Leader: Almighty God, our heavenly Father, who in his great mercy has promised forgiveness of sins to all those who sincerely repent and with true faith turn to him, have mercy upon you, pardon and deliver you from all your sins, confirm and strengthen you in all goodness, and bring you to everlasting life, through Jesus Christ our Lord. Amen.

For Pentecost

OPENING ACCLAMATION

Leader: You send forth your Spirit.

People: And renew the face of the earth.

SCRIPTURE

When the day of Pentecost came, they were all together in one place. Suddenly a sound like the blowing of a violent wind came from heaven and filled the whole house where they were sitting. They saw what seemed to be tongues of fire that separated and came to rest on each of them. All of them were filled with the Holy Spirit and began to speak in other tongues as the Spirit enabled them. (Acts 2:1-4)

Leader: The Word of the Lord.

People: Thanks be to God.

CALL AND RESPONSE

Leader: The Lord will pour out his Spirit upon all flesh,

People: And your sons and daughters shall prophesy.

Leader: Your old men shall dream dreams,

People: And your young men shall see visions.

Leader: You shall know that the Lord is in the midst of his people,

People: That he is the Lord and there is none else.

Leader: And it shall come to pass

People: That everyone who calls on the name of the Lord shall be saved.

A Franciscan Litany for Peace

Leader: Lord, make us instruments of your peace.
People: **Lord, hear our prayer.**

Leader: Where there is hatred, let us sow love;
People: **Lord, hear our prayer.**

Leader: where there is injury, pardon;
People: **Lord, hear our prayer.**

Leader: where there is discord, union;
People: **Lord, hear our prayer.**

Leader: where there is doubt, faith;
People: **Lord, hear our prayer.**

Leader: where there is despair, hope;
People: **Lord, hear our prayer.**

Leader: where there is darkness, light;
People: **Lord, hear our prayer.**

Leader: where there is sadness, joy.
People: **Lord, hear our prayer.**

Leader: Grant that we may not so much seek to be consoled as to console;
People: **Lord, hear our prayer.**

Leader: to be understood as to understand;
People: **Lord, hear our prayer.**

Leader: to be loved as to love.
People: **Lord, hear our prayer.**

Leader: For it is in giving that we receive;
People: **Lord, hear our prayer.**

Leader: it is in pardoning that we are pardoned;
People: **Lord, hear our prayer.**

Leader: and it is in dying that we are born to eternal life.
People: **Lord, hear our prayer.**
All: Amen.

Part 7
Table Blessings

Contemporary Blessings

For food and health and happy days
receive our gratitude and praise. Amen.

Thank you, God, for this food.
For rest and home.
And all things good.
For wind and rain and sun above.
But, most of all, those we love. Amen.

For food in a world where many walk in hunger;
For faith in a world where many walk in fear;
For friends in a world where many walk alone;
We give you thanks, O Lord. Amen.

Thank you for the food we eat,
Thank you for the world so sweet,
Thank you for the birds that sing,
Thank you, God, for everything. Amen.

God is great, God is good.
Let us thank him for our food.
By his hands, we are fed.
Let us thank him for our bread. Amen.

For this and all we are about to receive,
make us truly grateful, Lord.
Through Christ we pray, Amen.

For food that stays our hunger,
For rest that brings us ease,
For homes where memories linger,
We give our thanks for these. Amen.

For good food and
those who prepare it,
for good friends with whom to share it,
we thank you, Lord. Amen.

Lord, thank you for the food before us,
the family and friends beside us,
and the love between us. Amen.

Traditional Blessings

Bless, O Lord, this food to our use
and us to thy service, and
keep us ever mindful of the needs of others.
In Jesus' name, amen.

Be present at our table, Lord.
Be here and everywhere adored.
Thy people bless, and grant that we
may feast in paradise with Thee. Amen.
—John Wesley

Come, Lord Jesus, our guest to be
And bless these gifts
Bestowed by thee.
And bless our loved ones everywhere,
And keep them in your loving care. Amen.

Great God, our gratitude we bring,
Accept our humble offering,
For all the gifts on us bestowed,
Thy name be evermore adored. Amen.

Lord, bless this food and grant that we
May thankful for thy mercies be.
Teach us to know by whom we're fed;
Bless us with Christ, the living bread. Amen.

We thank you, God, for this our food,
for life and health and every good.
Let manna to our souls be given
the bread of life sent down from heaven. Amen.

We thank you, Lord, for all you give;
the food we eat, the lives we live;
and to our loved ones far away,
please send your blessings, Lord, we pray. Amen.

Bless us, oh Lord, and these thy gifts
which we are about to receive
from thy bounty through Christ our Lord. Amen.

Part 8
Prayers of the Saints

Prayers of the Saints

PRAYER OF CLEMENT OF ROME, 35-99

We beseech you, Master, to be our helper and protector. Save the afflicted among us; have mercy on the lowly; raise up the fallen; appear to the needy; heal the ungodly; restore the wanderers of thy people; feed the hungry; ransom our prisoners; raise up the sick; comfort the faint-hearted. Amen.

PRAYER OF ST. POLYCARP, 69-155

May God the Father, and the Eternal High Priest Jesus Christ, build us up in faith and truth and love, and grant to us our portion among the saints with all those who believe on our Lord Jesus Christ. We pray for all saints, for kings and rulers, for the enemies of the Cross of Christ, and for ourselves we pray that our fruit may abound and we may be made perfect in Christ Jesus our Lord. Amen.

PRAYER OF ST. IRENAEUS, 130-202

O Lamb of God, who takes away the sin of the world, look upon us and have mercy upon us; you who are yourself both victim and priest, yourself both reward and redeemer, keep safe from all evil those whom thou hast redeemed, O Savior of the world. Amen.

PRAYER OF ST. EPHREM OF SYRIA, 306-373

O Lord of my life, take away from me the spirit of laziness, faint-heartedness, lust for power and idle talk. Instead grant me, your servant, the spirit of purity, humility, patience and love. Yes, O Lord and King! Grant me to see my own sins and faults and not to judge my neighbor, for you are truly blessed forever. Amen.

PRAYER OF ST. CHRYSOSTOM, 347-407

Almighty God, who has given us at this time with one accord to make our common prayer to you; and does promise that when two or three are gathered together in your Name you will grant their request, fulfill now, O Lord, the desires and petitions of your servants, as may be most expedient for them; granting us in this world knowledge of thy truth; and in the world to come life everlasting. Amen.

PRAYER OF ST. JEROME, 342-420

Lord, you have given us your Word for a light to shine upon our path; grant us so to meditate on that Word, and to follow its teaching, that we may find in it the light that shines more and more until the perfect day, through Jesus Christ our Lord. Amen.

PRAYER OF ST. AUGUSTINE, 354-430

Breathe in me, O Holy Spirit, that my thoughts may all be holy. Act in me, O Holy Spirit, that my work, too, may be holy. Draw my heart, O Holy Spirit, that I love but what is holy. Strengthen me, O Holy Spirit, to defend all that is holy. Guard me, then, O Holy Spirit, that I always may be holy. Amen.

PRAYER OF ST. DIONYSIUS, C. 200-268

God the Father, source of everything Divine, You are good surpassing everything good and just surpassing everything just. In You is tranquility, as well as peace and harmony. Heal our divisions and restore us to the unity of love, which is similar to Your Divine nature. Let the bond of love and the ties of Divine affection make us one in the Spirit by your peace which renders everything peaceful. We ask this through the grace, mercy, and compassion of Your only Son, our Lord Jesus Christ. Amen.

PRAYER OF ST. PATRICK, 387-493

May the strength of God pilot me, the power of God uphold me, the wisdom of God guide me. May the eye of God look before me, the ear of God hear me, the Word of God speak for me. May the hand of God protect me, the way of God lie before me, the shield of God defend me, the host of God save me. May Christ shield me today. Christ with me, Christ before me, Christ behind me, Christ in me, Christ beneath me, Christ above me, Christ on my right, Christ on my left, Christ when I lie down, Christ when I sit, Christ when I stand, Christ in the heart of everyone who thinks of me, Christ in the mouth of everyone who speaks of me, Christ in every eye that sees me, Christ in every ear that hears me. Amen.

PRAYERS OF THE SAINTS

PRAYER OF ST. AUGUSTINE, 354-430

Look upon us, O Lord, and let all the darkness of our souls vanish before the beams of your brightness. Fill us with holy love, and open to us the treasures of thy wisdom. All our desire is known unto you, therefore perfect what you have begun, and what your Spirit has awakened us to ask in prayer. We seek your face; turn your face unto us and show us your glory. Then shall our longing be satisfied, and our peace shall be perfect. Amen.

PRAYER OF ST. AMBROSE OF MILAN, 339-397

O Lord, who hast mercy upon all, take away from me my sins, and mercifully kindle in me the fire of thy Holy Spirit. Take away from me the heart of stone, and give me a heart of flesh, a heart to love and adore you, a heart to delight in you, to follow and to enjoy you, for Christ's sake. Amen.

PRAYER OF ST. JEROME, 342-420

O good shepherd, seek me out, and bring me home to your fold again. Deal favorably with me according to thy good pleasure, till I may dwell in your house all the days of my life, and praise you forever and ever with them that are there. Amen.

PRAYER OF ST. BENEDICT, 480-547

Gracious and holy Father, give me wisdom to perceive you, intelligence to fathom you, patience to wait for you, eyes to behold you, a heart to meditate upon you, and a life to proclaim you, through the power of the Spirit of Jesus Christ our Lord. Amen.

PRAYER OF ST. COLUMBA, 521-597

Alone with none but you, my God, I journey on my way. What need I fear, when you are near, O king of night and day? More safe am I within your hand than if a host did round me stand. Amen.

PRAYER OF ST. AIDAN, ?-651

Leave me alone with God as much as may be. As the tide draws the waters close in upon the shore, make me an island, set apart, alone with you, God, holy to you. Then with the turning of the tide prepare me to carry your presence to the busy world beyond, the world that rushes in on me till the waters come again and fold me back to you. Amen.

PRAYER OF ST. CAEDMON, 658-680

Now let me praise the keeper of Heaven's kingdom, the might of the Creator, and his thought, the work of the Father of glory, how each of wonders the Eternal Lord established in the beginning. He first created for the sons of men Heaven as a roof, the holy Creator, then Middle- earth the keeper of mankind, the Eternal Lord, afterwards made, the earth for men, the Almighty Lord. Amen.

PRAYER OF ST. ALCUIN, 735-804

Eternal Light, shine into our hearts; Eternal Goodness, deliver us from evil; Eternal Power, be our support; Eternal Wisdom, scatter the darkness of our ignorance: That we may seek Your face with all our heart and mind and soul and strength. Amen.

PRAYER OF ST. THOMAS À KEMPIS, 1380-1470

Lord, You know what is best; let this be done or that be done as You please. Give what You will, as much as You will, when You will. Do with me as You know best, as will most please You, and will be for Your greater honor. Place me where You will and deal with me freely in all things. I am in Your hand; turn me about whichever way You will. Behold, I am Your servant, ready to obey in all things. Not for myself do I desire to live, but for You—would that I could do this worthily and perfectly! Amen.

PRAYER OF ST. ANSELM, 1033-1109

Lord, because you have made me, I owe you the whole of my love; because you have redeemed me, I owe you the whole of myself; because you have promised so much, I owe you my whole being. Moreover, I owe you as much more love than myself as you are greater than I, for whom you gave yourself and to whom you promised yourself. I pray you, Lord, make me taste by love what I taste by knowledge; let me know by love what I know by understanding. I owe you more than my whole self, but I have no more, and by myself I cannot render the whole of it to you. Draw me to you, Lord, in the fullness of your love. I am wholly yours by creation; make me all yours, too, in love. Amen.

PRAYER OF ST. BERNARD OF CLAIRVAUX, 1090-1153

Jesus, the very thought of you with sweetness fills the breast; But sweeter far your face to see, And in your presence rest. Nor voice can sing, nor heart can frame, Nor can the memory find a sweeter sound than your blessed Name, O Savior of mankind! O hope of every contrite heart, O joy of all the meek, To those who fall, how kind you are! How good to those who seek! O Jesus, light of all below, fount of living fire, surpassing all the joys we know, and all we can desire. Abide with us, and let your light shine, Lord, on every heart; Dispel the darkness of our night; And joy to all impart. Amen.

PRAYER OF ST. FRANCIS, 1181-1226

Lord, make me an instrument of your peace. Where there is hatred, let me sow love; where there is injury, pardon; where there is doubt, faith; where there is despair, hope; where there is darkness, light; and where there is sadness, joy. O Divine Master, grant that I may not so much seek to be consoled as to console; to be understood as to understand; to be loved as to love. For it is in giving that we receive; it is in pardoning that we are pardoned; and it is in dying that we are born to eternal life. Amen.

PRAYER OF ST. CLARE OF ASSISI, 1194-1253

Place your mind before the mirror of eternity! Place your soul in the brilliance of glory! Place your heart in the figure of the divine substance! And transform your whole being into the image of the Godhead Itself through contemplation! So that you too may feel what His friends feel as they taste the hidden sweetness which God Himself has reserved from the beginning for those who love Him. Amen.

PRAYER OF ST. THOMAS AQUINAS, 1225-1274

Grant me, O Lord my God, a mind to know you, a heart to seek you, wisdom to find you, conduct pleasing to you, faithful perseverance in waiting for you, and a hope of finally embracing you. Amen.

PRAYER OF ST. CATHERINE OF SIENA, 1347-1380

O eternal Trinity, with the light of understanding I have tasted and seen the depths of your mystery and the beauty of your creation. In seeing myself in you, I have seen that I will become like you. O eternal Father, from your power and your wisdom clearly you have given to me a share of that wisdom which belongs to Thine only-begotten Son. And truly have the Holy Spirit, who proceeds from you, Father and Son, given to me the desire to love you. O eternal Trinity, you are my maker and I am your creation. Illuminated by you, I have learned that you have made me a new creation through the blood of your only begotten Son because you are captivated by love at the beauty of your creation. Amen.

PRAYER OF ST. IGNATIUS LOYOLA, 1491-1556

Soul of Christ, sanctify me. Body of Christ, save me. Blood of Christ, inebriate me. Water from the side of Christ, wash me. Passion of Christ, strengthen me. O good Jesus, hear me. Within thy sacred wounds hide me. From the wicked enemy defend me. In the hour of my death call me and bid me come to thee, that with thy saints I may praise thee forever and ever. Amen.

PRAYER OF LANCELOT ANDREWES, 1555-1600

Be all to all. We bring before You, O God, the cries of the weary, the pains of the distressed, the tears of the tragedies of life, the anxious hours of the insecure, the restlessness of the refugees, the hunger of the oppressed. Dear God, be near to each. Helper of the helpless, Hope of the homeless, The Strength of those tossed with tempests, The Haven of those who sail, Be all to all. Be within us, to strengthen us; without us, to keep us; above us, to inspire us; beneath us, to uphold us; before us, to direct us; behind us, to propel us; around us, to sustain us. Be all to all in present need. Amen.

PRAYER OF ST. JOHN HENRY NEWMAN, 1801-1890

Dear Jesus, help me to spread your fragrance everywhere I go; Flood my soul with your spirit and life; Penetrate and possess my whole being so completely that all my life may be only a radiance of yours; Shine through me and be so in me that everyone with whom I come into contact may feel your presence within me. Let them look up and see no longer me—but only Jesus. Amen.

Recommended Reading

Adam, David. *The Edge of Glory: Prayers in the Celtic Tradition*. London: SPCK Publishing, 2011.

Benson, Robert. *Constant Prayer*. Nashville: Thomas Nelson, 2009.

Bevins, Winfield. *A Field Guide to Daily Prayer*. Franklin, TN: Seedbed Publishing, 2015.

———. *A Field Guide to Family Prayer*. Franklin, TN: Seedbed Publishing, 2019.

Black, Vicki K. *Welcome to the Book of Common Prayer*. Harrisburg, PA: Morehouse Publishing, 2005.

The Book of Common Prayer, New York: Church Publishing, 1979.

The Book of Common Prayer, Huntington Beach, CA: Anglican Liturgical Press, 2019.

Bradshaw, Paul F. *Daily Prayer in the Early Church: A Study of the Origin and Early Development of the Divine Office*. Eugene, OR: Wipf & Stock Publishers, 2008.

Carey, George. *Celebrating Common Prayer*. New York: Continuum, 1999.

Chittister, Joan. *The Liturgical Year*. Nashville: Thomas Nelson, 2009.

Community of Jesus. *The Little Book of Hours: Praying with the Community of Jesus*. Brewster, MA: Paraclete Press, 2007.

Galli, Mark. *Beyond Smells and Bells: The Wonder and Power of Christian Liturgy*. Brewster, MA: Paraclete Press, 2008.

Hatchett, Marion J. *Commentary on the American Prayer Book*. New York: The Seabury Press, 1981.

Lee, Jeffrey. *Opening the Prayer Book: The New Church's Teaching Series*, Vol 7. Cambridge, MA: Crowley Publications, 1999.

McKnight, Scot. *Praying with the Church: Following Jesus, Daily, Hourly, Today*. Brewster, MA: Paraclete Press, 2006.

Merton, Thomas. *A Book of Hours*. Notre Dame, IN: Sorin Books, 2007.

RECOMMENDED READING

Newell, J. Philip. *Celtic Benediction: Morning and Night Prayer.* Grand Rapids, MI: Eerdmans Publishing, 2000.

Northumbria Community. *Celtic Daily Prayer: Prayers and Readings from the Northumbria Community.* New York: HarperOne, 2002.

Saint Benedict's Prayer Book for Beginners. Ampleforth Abbey, York, UK: Ampleforth Abbey Press, 1994.

Snyder, Howard A. *Prayers for Ordinary Days.* Franklin, TN: Seedbed Publishing, 2018.

Sydnor, William. *The Study of the Real Prayer Book: 1549 to the Present.* Wilton, CT: Morehouse Publishing, 1978.

Tickle, Phyllis. *The Divine Hours: Prayers for Autumn and Winter.* New York: Doubleday Books. 2000.

———. *The Divine Hours: Prayers for Springtime.* New York: Doubleday Books. 2000.

———. *The Divine Hours: Prayers for Summertime.* New York: Doubleday Books. 2000.

Wainwright, Geoffrey & Karen B. Westerfield Tucker, eds. *The Oxford History of Christian Worship.* Oxford/New York: Oxford University Press, 2006.

Warren, Tish Harrison. *The Liturgy of the Ordinary: Sacred Practices in Everyday Life.* Downers Grove, IL: IVP Books, 2016.